The Seven Secrets of Great Walmart People Greeters

A Job Hunting Book by

Joseph Corey III

Cinedyne Press

Copyright © 2012 Joseph Corey III

All rights reserved.

ISBN-13:
978-1479314140

LEGAL DISCLAIMER

The Seven Secrets of Great Walmart People Greeters is not an official publication of Walmart Stores Inc. Walmart Stores Inc. did not authorize, sanction, cooperate or contribute to the content of this book. Walmart is a registered trademark of Walmart Stores Inc. *The Seven Secret*s are not based on any known training material used by Walmart Stores Inc.

Memorizing *The Seven Secrets* will not automatically guarantee the reader will be hired as a Walmart People Greeter. *The Seven Secrets* shouldn't hurt your chances of gaining the desired position.

The Seven Secrets can be applied to any business that has a greeter position such as large hardware stores, megachurches and casinos.

CONTENTS

Dedication   i

Introduction   1

Secret One   11

Secret Two   21

Secret Three   39

Secret Four   55

Secret Five   75

Secret Six   97

Secret Seven   111

Final Exam   123

Dedicated to my wife
for letting me live the dream every day.

"Welcome to Walmart!"
                              The Future You

SO YOU WANT TO BE A WALMART PEOPLE GREETER

This was not supposed to be your destiny.

What mature person stares down at a job application to be a Walmart People Greeter with giddy anticipation? This isn't the dream job topper of a glamorous career like becoming a sports historian, consultant at a hedge fund or taste tester at an ice cream factory. This isn't the first step on the journey to be an astronaut, brain surgeon or media mogul. A teen landing his first real paycheck at a fast food joint knows he's paying his dues and priming the pump for success. People Greeter is not an envied title to have at the top of a resume. Kindergartners cry if they're assigned to play the People Greeter while all the other kids shop in a fake store. Nobody gets this position listed as his top choice on a high school occupational interest test. Community colleges don't offer it as a major. Who would take such a course willingly? Most folks consider People Greeter as the step taken before entering a hospice. Why would anyone want to spend their final days on Earth telling strangers, "Welcome to Walmart" and meaning it?

Because this is the most visible job option for people looking for work who have been out of college for a few decades.

People Greeter at Walmart is one of the few positions in America actively filled by people over 50. Fifty has become the un-magic number when employers no longer view employees as viable. Aged workers are a drag on efficiency, company insurance and pay rates in an employer's minds. TV networks view anyone 50 and older as a detriment to their programming. Nobody wants to be the senior citizens station. This is a youth worshipping culture. Older employees are deadweight in today's corporations. Job postings want the person with the most experience and the youngest age. The only other positions desiring mature applicants are Santa and Mrs. Claus at shopping malls. Being St. Nick or his wife sounds like respected positions for senior citizens. But what are you going to do for a living between December 26 and Thanksgiving Day? You're not considering a job that's seasonal. The bills arrive all year long. You can work as a Walmart People Greeter for 365 days (and 366 days in Leap Years).

There are three types of people considering being Walmart People Greeters that never imagined this as an option for the end of their working lives. None of them can be described as major screw ups who wasted their better years with foolish indulgences and vices. They were people that were serious about their careers. They worked at a real company and cared about their retirement. When it comes to the story of the grasshopper and the ant, they were ants. They understood obligations, work ethic and loyalty. They could pass a drug test. Who are these three types and which one is you?

Unexpected

The first group started their last day of work as merely another day to be scratched off the calendar on the march towards a gold watch. Before making breakfast, they were already contemplating which restaurant would get their business lunch action. They showed up at their desk a little early and prepared to put in an honest day's work for the company. Then the bottom fell out with a message to drop by the supervisor's office. After decades on the job, their final minutes are spent with a strange face from Human Resources informing them that they're the victims of companywide layoffs. The pink slip had nothing to do with their own performance. The company needed to streamline the workforce so it can proceed in a more efficient direction. Their old department can be handled by contract employees in Bangalore, India. The employer acts like it's a comforting thought for the freshly unemployed that at least it's not a younger version of themselves stealing their job.

What will the freshly laid off do since they're years away from touching their retirement funds? They'll contact their opposite number at rival companies. Odds are high that their rival has also had their position outsourced or eliminated as part of the herd mentality within management. The unemployed will call up headhunters and post their resume online. Then they wait. They might get nibbles. Numerous hoops in the interview process torture them. How many phone calls will a company require before they even consider a site visit for a formal meeting? The process can drag for weeks and months with the final decision arriving in the mail like all bad news. The letter explains that the company had so many talented candidates and unfortunately they didn't get the job. The heartbreak just never ends. The truly unfortunate will be stuck with a non-compete clause in their contract. Can they afford to sit around for a year or more waiting to work in their old profession? What good is someone who has been out of the loop that long? By the time they get hired, they're going to have to learn a whole new system. Are the laid off eager to retrain themselves for a fresh occupation? It's just easier for a company to hire fresh out of college kids and train them the first time around. What are the odds that their brilliant new career can't also be done cheaper across the ocean?

Many think that lack of interested employers is a blessing in disguise. They believe this is the perfect time to start their own business. But not everyone wants to put up with the burdens that come with entrepreneurship. They can't deal with the headaches and heartbreaks of a start-up business. If they were really ready to be an entrepreneur, they would have quit their job to pursue their dream instead of waiting for the axe. They would be reading *How to Get Instantly Rich with Your Own Business* instead of *The Seven Secrets of Great Walmart People Greeters*. Most laid off workers merely want to get their career back on the tracks. This is not as simple as when they were younger cause back there they had what employers want — youth.

After all the rejection, they redefine their goal to a job that can tide them over until they can tap their retirement nest egg without harsh penalties. They contemplate the one position for mature applicants that doesn't require kids sitting on their laps.

Broken Eggs

The second group is those who discover their retirement nest eggs have cracked. These were not foolish people that skimped on investing a portion of their paycheck into a 401(K) or IRA. Back in the '80s, they were taking care of their future self when by setting up retirement plans that were supposedly better than traditional company pensions. They let financial advisors set up a worry free system that allowed them to forget about such worries and enjoy cruising around in a Fiero to a *Miami Vice* party with the promise of wine coolers upon arrival. According to the hype, the new "pension" plans would be worth millions when an employee chose to retire. What never got quite explained was that results might vary. Dramatic shifts can occur thanks to stock market collapses, corporate bankruptcies and deceptive financial advisors. Even people with traditional pension plans are not immune from being financially devastated. Companies implode their pension plans in bankruptcy reorganizations.

While the Pension Benefit Guaranty Corporation is supposed to act as a safety net, their funds have been hit hard over the last decade. Retirees find themselves receiving a fraction of their previous pension check. This lack of funding puts a major dent in the act of doing nothing all day. The retirees need a job that supplements the loss of nest-egg revenue, but they don't want to really go back to work. How much work can it be to welcome people to a store?

Ironmen

The third group is those who can't enjoy being retired. They swore when they were employed that they'd spend their golden years doing all the stuff that they never got around to doing because of work. They discovered after a week into retirement that they really never wanted to do any of that stuff. Puttering around the house, shuffleboarding on a cruise ship and hanging out at the senior center gives them an empty feeling. They miss being part of the work force. They need to clock in, feel responsible and be active. Why don't these people volunteer at a charity to stay busy? Perhaps they'd rather not worry about fundraising and donors? Or their puritan work ethic includes receiving a paycheck for their day's work. What matter to them is they need a job that feels like they're contributing as an employee. They don't want to worry about a forced retirement age. People Greeters have been known to celebrate 100th birthdays during their shifts at Walmart. The job doesn't have to end until they're really ready to do nothing all day. They perceive the position as close to doing nothing all day so it'd be an easy transition.

Did you find your situation in the three types? That's nice, but it really doesn't matter what made you to contemplate the position of Walmart People Greeter. What matters is that all three types perceive the job as one that can fit their needs from their encounters with People Greeters over the years. But do they really understand the position's history and responsibilities?

History of the People Greeter

The People Greeter appears to be a throwback to 1880s commerce. They would have worn straw hats and blue vests while working at the front of a dry goods store. The Greeter welcomed customers riding up in their buggies. They eagerly hitched up the horses near the water trough. They directed the customers to the jars of mustache wax, jugs of sarsaparilla and bolts of gingham. They joined together with three other employees in a barbershop quartet to provide happy shopping music. Was this a tradition reborn when the first Walmart was opened in 1962 to give a nostalgic atmosphere to the new shopping experience? Turns out the People Greeter aren't a traditional retail position from bygone days or even from Walmart's grand opening.

Its history merely extends back to early 1980s. Stories of the creation of the Walmart People Greeter vary. One has a regular employee sending founder Sam Walton a suggestion note that stores should have an employee near the front doors to welcome customers and catch shoplifters. Another claims that Sam Walton was greeted at a store in Louisiana by a People Greeter. The manager wanted customers to feel good when they enter the store. Sam fell in love with concept and made it a companywide policy. The final theory is that store managers wanted to cut back on the rate of shoplifting. They were eager to hire security guards to stand by the front of the door. Sam wanted something friendlier than armed guards. Which one is true? Hard to definitively say, but the truth is probably a mixture of the three narratives.

A show of force in the form of an armed guard at the front of a store always puts customers on edge. The innocent shopper gets nervous that they might be shopping in a dangerous place. What sorts of people are going to be near their shopping cart and children? Security Guards also prove to be rather inefficient when it comes to being employees. They must keep their eyes peeled for suspects. Their hands must be free so they can draw their gun at a moment's notice. They're just going to stand by the entrance holding up the wall for eight hours. Walmart prefers active employees during their shifts that can do more than stare. The stores needed a way to make shoplifters not think the front entrance was unattended, shoppers feel welcomed and employees weren't paid to stand around. The People Greeter proved to be the perfect compromise.

The People Greeter had numerous tasks when the position was rolled out at the Walmarts across America in 1983. They weren't hired to merely be a store fixture. Their responsibilities included:s

- Greet incoming customers. Everyone should feel welcomed when they step inside the store.

- Give customers shopping carts, baskets or wheelchairs.

- Towel dry the carts on rainy days.

- Keep the entrance clean. All garbage that ended up on the floor needed to quickly go in the garbage cans. Nobody wants to enter a dirty store. Customers are also notorious for opening items on their way out and paying no attention if the packaging is properly disposed.

- Wash the front doors when the glass got smudged.

- Direct customers to items.

- Adjust displays near the entrance so products are orderly and facing the front of the shelf.

- Hand out Walmart promotional stickers to small children.

- Mark and log items being returned by customers. This is a way of proving the customer really brought the item into the store. Scam artists will enter the store with a receipt, grab an item off the shelf, sneak the up to the customer service desk and demand a cash refund since it's on the receipt.

- Thank outgoing shoppers for visiting the store.

- Check customer's receipts if they leave with large items that won't fit in a bag or set off the security gate.

- Report any suspicious customers to a loss prevention associate.

That's a full day for one person's shift. There's no time to lean up against a wall and eyeball customers to spot a potential troublemaker. People Greeters were busy bees as they did so much around the entrance and still found time to welcome so many. This tremendous amount of duties might scare people looking for the perfect late in life job. Don't let the list scare you from applying for the position.

Over the decades, the duties of the Walmart People Greeter have been reduced. What's expected of the People Greeter varies by store. Rarely are People Greeters positioned near the shopping carts in the superstores. They no longer fear tweaking their backs while separating locked carts to hand them off to customers.

Certain stores allow the People Greeters to have a stool near their workstation so they can take a seat during slow times. There are stores that require the People Greeter to write out information about returned items in a notebook while others have a handheld scanner perform the heavy work.

The best thing you can do is visit all the Walmarts in your area to get a sense of the People Greeters duties. Casually observe them while you're shopping near the entrance. You might be bold enough to ask them what their job entails. Don't tell them the truth if they want to know why you're asking about their job. Nobody likes to meet the person that hopes to replace him. Let them know you're merely a curious person. Thank them for making you feel welcomed when you visit the store. What's important is to pick your favorite store and a safety store before beginning the application process. This is just like college except you won't get calls for alumni fundraising drives.

Why do you need to buy this book and study the Seven Secrets to be hired for a job that's a flight of steps down from your previous position? Being a People Greeter seems rather easy. You don't need a PhD, a medical license and a reference letter from the President of the United States of America to stand at the entrance. What can possibly justify buying this book and studying the pages?

Because you need a competitive advantage.

There's nearly 4,300 Walmarts across America, which sounds like plenty of People Greeter positions are available. Every day thousands of people find themselves in your situation. You're not the only person considering becoming a People Greeter at this very moment. Not everyone with grey hair, glasses and a completely filled out application can immediately join the Walmart family. Hundreds of people every day are rejected because just looking good in navy blue and khaki isn't good enough. The competition for the position is getting tougher as the number of People Greeter positions are shrinking. Stores have reduced the shift hours so the People Greeter mainly works during peak shopping times. Managers have been altering the responsibilities. The People Greeter station has been posited farther back from the store so they can direct shoppers to waiting cashiers. You shouldn't give up hope that the position is going to be completely be eliminated like your last job.

How does this differ from applying for any other job in a shrinking market? Your resume won't be tossed aside because it hints that you're not fresh out of college. These changes to the People Greeter position mean that you must be a serious candidate when you deliver your job application and not someone who thinks it looks easy. You must appear prepared with the right attitude and mental tools for the job. The Seven Secrets will allow anyone in the hiring process to sense that you're only a nametag short of being a People Greeter.

The Seven Secrets are not shortcuts or cheat codes. If you're expecting quick and painless answers that will fool your future boss, look for another book with fewer pages and more illustrations. The Seven Secrets are not part of a poster handed out during corporate training at Walmart. The Seven Secrets were revealed from observation and casual interviews with numerous People Greeters that were considered the pride of their stores. None were formally interviewed because it was important to understand how they act and react during their shifts. There was no need for them to repeat what they remembered from the employee handbook. The Seven Secrets represent traits, habits and mindsets that elevated these Greeters into Great Greeters. Accepting these Seven Secrets will allow you to embrace the enjoyable parts of the position while not being overwhelmed by the more frustrating elements.

The Seven Secrets will also let you know if you're really ready to be a People Greeter. If the position isn't a right fit, you need to immediately start working on a Santa suit and growing a beard. You already have a fragile psyche after being fired and struggling to land another job. The last thing you need to discover is that you can't cut it as a People Greeter. You've already had to humble yourself to consider the position. Can you stomach the shame of being released during the probationary period? If you can't master the Seven Secrets, this is not the job for you. The position is harder than it appears if done right.

It's only easy if you want to be a Bad People Greeter. There's only one secret to being a bad People Greeter and it can be summed up in two words: Don't care. The bad People Greeters don't care about welcoming customers. They don't care about being attentive. They wander away from their station to see what other employees are doing. You can't afford to be a bad People Greeter. You have no desire to be scolded like an indifferent junior high student or given a second pink slip in less than a year. The Seven Secrets provide a way to be respected when you're stationed at the entrance.

Maybe being a Walmart People Greeter isn't how you imagined ending your working career, but the Seven Secrets will allow you to realize this is a perfect way to wind down to retirement. This isn't that bleak and demeaning of a final act. The future will be bright if you desire to be a Great Walmart Greeter using the Seven Secrets. The Seven Secrets will empower you and instill you with pride when you tell an incoming customer, "Welcome to Walmart."

SECRET ONE: BE A PEOPLE PERSON

A job interviewer always asks a potential employee his or her best traits. The interviewee usually reels off a list of pleasing qualities before finally declaring, "I'm a people person!" How many times have you tossed that phrase at a potential employer? It flows off the tongue easily. The statement makes things end on an extremely positive and pleasing note. Who doesn't want a "People Person" instead of a Malignant Misanthrope? Ultimately this classic cliché is a coded way of saying, "I need this job badly. Please, please, please give me this job before I have to get out of this chair and go home and wait by the phone for days until I realize you've merely sent me a postcard saying you had so many great applicants and I wasn't the winner. I don't want to have to worry about what I am going to do for the rest of my life. You're my last hope." In other words, it's a polite cry for help.

You can't lie about your ability to be a people person when you apply to be a People Greeter. "People" is in the job title. This job won't be a good fit if you can only work alone with your office door locked and a secretary telling callers, "They're in a meeting."

You really have to enjoy encountering people to do this gig. It's like begging to be a swim coach when you have a deathly fear of water or a doctor when you faint at the sight of blood. The average Walmart store has around 41,000 customers enter its front doors during the week. A full-time greeter doesn't merely observe this horde of humanity, but interacts with them. Think back to your previous position; did you have the same number of people that attend a mid-major college football game knock on your door each week? Are your palms getting a little sweaty thinking of that rush of shoppers emerging from the electric front doors? Take a deep breath. Don't get too nervous since they'll be spaced over seven days. Although there is a fierce chance that 41,000 might all rush past you on Black Friday when the doors crack open at 3 a.m.

Founder Sam Walton made employees take a pledge that if there was a customer within 10 feet; their immediate response was to look him or her in the eye, welcome him or her to the store and ask if he or she need assistance. Walmart is not an exclusive boutique where the staff ignores the clientele until they prove worthy of receiving their service. There's no pouting when a person has a question that interrupts your daydreams or texting your grandkids. You can't hide in the stockroom waiting for the people to go home. If you have that attitude, do not waste your time filling out the application. You must be all about the people.

Stranger Person

You have to be more than a People Person to succeed in this role. You have to be a Stranger Person. What's the difference? A People Person "knows" the people they're associating with. It takes that rare person who can start a conversation with a complete stranger. Think of the last time you rode in an elevator. Do you remember the people who shared the ride? Did you have a conversation with any of them that wasn't merely asking them politely to press the button for your floor? Did you feel the need to introduce yourself or ask them about their day? A majority of folks remain silent during the ride. They either look at the floor numbers flashing away or their feet. There's no shoe gazing when you pin on your employee badges and assume the position. This job is not made for shy people. You can't be nervous at the prospect of strangers making eye contact. You are not allowed to look down and mumble your greeting. There are only three reasons your eye-line should ever connect with the floor: Someone has dropped something; There's a mess that needs to be cleaned up; Or to detect a barefoot customer.

This is not an ideal position if you have a panic attack when forced to speak to a human operator on the phone. This is not a great position if you suffer fits of paranoia. You can't calm your fears because they are partially true. People are looking at you. They will act like they know you when they ask information about the store. They expect you to greet them as if they're not strangers. You might not be cut out for the position if your first reaction to a stranger knowing your name is to flee the room. How would they know your name? During a shift, you are required to wear a nametag. Most people won't notice it, but a few customers will address you by your first name to make it seem like a warm conversation. Can you handle that? They might ask if where you've been if you took a few days off. Don't panic.

Under the Microscope

The security camera is trained on your position so all of your actions are being followed. Management may evaluate your performance based on video footage. If a customer complains about something you did, they'll go to the tapes. Can you handle that much attention? Thousands are watching you like a TV star.

Germaphobes will find the position a challenge. You'll encounter people with various degrees of hygiene that will get in your personal space. You may be touched by the unwashed masses since they might be grateful for your help and shake your hand. Are you cringing at that thought? Even more threatening will be customers in various stages of sickness eager for directions to the pharmacy section. You're going to know when the first phlegm ball is coughed up for flu season. How do you react when a stranger sneezes near you? Now imagine them unloading their nasal mist directly at you. Can you remain at your station without wanting to constantly race into the bathroom to coat your body in hand sanitizer every five minutes? They don't want you using up all the wipes meant for the shopping cart handles. This is a job for people who don't mind such ugliness. You might want to invest in a yearly flu shot.

High Tolerance

Racists and bigots need not apply. This is not a job for you if you have major issues with certain races, cultures, sexual orientation or religions. You will encounter people of all walks of life as you stand in front of the entrance. This is not a snooty restaurant or haughty nightclub with a velvet rope outside to block the undesirables. The world shops at Walmart. Thus you must embrace all kinds. You have to treat everyone with warmth and acceptance. Ask yourself what would Jesus or Sammy Davis Jr. do? You can't give any group of people a distrustful eye. You can't have your voice change tone to mark your displeasure in a customer stepping past you. You might think you can disguise your inner feelings, but that wad of hate trapped in your throat will spew out. Maybe not in your words, but in your actions and expressions. People will notice you have a different attitude towards them when compared with the person you greeted before them. Everyone must be treated as an equal. The only exception is children. Be extra nice to them for they are future Walmart shoppers who need nurturing.

There are no exceptions as to who gets a welcome. Over 176 million people visit Wal-Mart each week. Odds are high not everyone will be acceptable to you bigoted sensibilities. Can you overcome your prejudice or do you sense that constant exposure will harden your hatred? Hopefully you view this as a way to make yourself a better and more accepting person.

Rise Above It

The job humbles you. How can you view yourself as superior to people when they're the shopper and you're the person in the khaki and navy blue vest ushering them inside? You have no authority over people. You can't make their lives any harder or put fear into them like a DMV employee. The worse you can do is not welcome them into the building. If word gets back to your superior that you're constantly ignoring Sam Walton's 10-foot rule, you'll be the one who will feel the consequences. Remember that you are not tenured into this position. Every day there are more people in your same circumstances that consider being a People Greeter as their best option for a late life career. You can always be replaced by a friendlier People Person.

Far as you're concerned people can only be divided up into two different groups: Cash or Charge. You may also refer to them as paper and plastic since this no longer refers to a customer's bagging choice. There are a few customers who will want to write a check. Those people are freaks. Odds are they're buying sugar and apples for their horse and buggy tied up in the parking lot. Thankfully, you won't have to deal with them spending five minutes deciding what to write in the memo slot. Their line jamming payment source is reserved for the cashiers. You merely have to inform them what identification they need to provide to cash a check when they're done pushing the shopping buggy around the store. Conversely a greeter must have thick skin because he or she might be the subject of racism and bigotry from arriving customers. You might give the nicest welcome and they'll throw back a slur under their breath as they march past you. Don't escalate this poor attitude by questioning what they just called you. That's just the sad nature of people who sometimes hate you and there's nothing you can do about it. It's not your job to cure them of their ways. You don't have the time to prove their preset notions are foolish and hateful. You've got to greet the person one step behind them. Part of being a people person is to just avoid thinking of people as individuals. Don't over think the position. You lived up to your end of the bargain by greeting them and making sure they weren't bringing a returned item into the store. Don't take their reaction as an attack. There's a chance you might have misheard them or they could have Tourette's syndrome. The last thing you need to do is create an issue out of a misunderstanding or neuropyschiatric disorder. Your first reaction to a perceived slurs should never be shouting, "Why don't you say that to my face?" You are in the People Greeter's position because of your maturity. You weren't hired to act like the hooligan eager to start a fight at a dive bar. You are a people greeter and not a people beater.

Now this does not mean that you should believe that everyone who enters the store is pure of heart with innocent intention. There are thousands of sweet and honest people visiting your store. But like the massive display of shining golden delicious apples, you must stay alert for the occasional worm. You should remember that there are those sinister people who plot and scheme against the store. If you spot a customer that has many of the telltale signs of a shoplifter (as instructed to you by the Asset Protection Manager), don't hesitate to point him out to your contact in the store security (Asset Protection Team). Make sure you pick that suspect out based completely off warning signs from your training and not merely cause you don't trust their "kinda people." You can't afford to be known as the Greeter who singles out a certain race, culture or religion when you contact security. You must be willing to spot the shoplifters from every race, culture and religion. No group has a monopoly on scheming and deceiving when it comes to claiming a five-finger discount. Remember to greet the suspects the same way you do the presumed innocent customers. You can't let them know they've been marked.

The Right Stuff

How can you truly tell if you're a People Person and not a People Pretender? You may think you've got experience, but have you really put yourself out there? There are plenty of ways to get your feet wet. Show up early at a sporting event and stand near the main entrance. Don't block traffic. Act like you're waiting on a friend who is running late. Experience the wave after wave of people as they file past you on their way to the metal detector. You need to stand straight and look people in the eyes as if you're hunting for your special friend. If anyone stares back, give a short wave. If event security asks what you're doing, tell them say you're waiting on your buddy who has your tickets. This way when the event starts, you can go home if you're not into the game. Examine the experience on the drive home. Did you feel embarrassed or shameful as the last people trickled inside? Did you want to come up with excuses if a stranger stared back? Were you more shy as the night wore on or did you get bolder eyeballing all the new faces? Did you feel natural just giving them a slight greeting when required? A People Person should never feel unnatural or overwhelmed in such a situation. If you're a little uncertain, repeat this exercise two or ten more times. If you need the extra practice, you might want to buy a ticket for a few of the games or stadium security might peg you as a weirdo and have you questioned by the off-duty cops for your suspicious activities. Ultimately there is nothing suspicious in your activities because you are preparing yourself for the moment when you can proudly declare, "I'm a People Person." For the first time in your life, it won't be a desperate cry for help.

POP QUIZ

1) List all the races, cultures and religions you despise:

_____

_____

_____

_____

_____

2) What diseases do you fear catching from strangers?

_____

_____

_____

_____

_____

3) Can you only work with your office door locked?

_____.

4) Are you a People Person with only people you already know?

_____.

The Seven Secrets of Great Walmart People Greeters

ANSWER KEY

If you gave an answer besides "No" or "None" to any of the questions, you might want to find a different job.

SECRET TWO: BE WELCOMING

The primary duty of a Walmart People Greeter is conveniently found in the job title: greet people. It's that simple. Don't break a sweat thinking there's a *Beautiful Mind* cryptogram hidden in there. There's no confusing tail chasing mix of words to befuddle outsiders like BI architect, vice president of digital strategy, custodial engineer or regional director of district supervisors. Feel the mental relief of not having to explain your primary duty after declaring your title after decades of dealing with sneaky resume positions that don't even come close to describing the occupational responsibilities. The People Greeter greets people. The people greeter lets the customers know that they're welcomed into the store with a human element instead of a sun-bleached "Welcome" sign dangling on the front door that transforms into "Closed."

The act of greeting leads to a key trait that separates applicants with People Greeter aspirations: Can you make a stranger feel welcomed? Not just one stranger, but also hundreds and thousands of them over your shift. It's harder than you imagine if you've never found yourself in such a situation.

When was the last time you looked a complete stranger in the eye and welcomed him to your work place? The substitute water cooler technicians and recently hired coworkers on their first day in the office don't count. Been a while, right? Or maybe you can't remember it ever happening. Don't feel shame in lacking this experience. It's not completely your fault.

High tech security and "no solicitors" signs insured that strangers never got near your office or approached you on the factory floor. Random people didn't wander through the front doors, down the hallways and poke their head in private offices with the excuse of just browsing. Security gates established that nobody drove into the parking lot without the right pass. Badges, codes and cameras only allowed properly authorized people to enter the workplace. This fortress atmosphere prevented homicidal, disgruntled ex-employees from settling scores. You knew exactly who was coming to see you during the workday. The receptionist called to let you know a guest was waiting for you in the lobby. Strangers were not welcomed. Think of the times you visited an office on business. We're you always welcomed when you got in the front door? How many times did you wait to be acknowledged while a receptionist finished off a private phone call? When she finally got done, she grilled you about why you had to disturb her routine. Who did you need to see? Did you have an appointment? What was the purpose of wanting to see the person? Were you expected? Or was it merely a no-nonsense security guard that pointed to a clipboard for you write down your name, business and why you had to come through their front door so they didn't have to listen to your story. Either way, you were not permitted to enter without revealing details about yourself. They eventually handed you a tag that identified you before letting you enter. They don't want strangers beyond that point.

This treatment of strangers isn't merely a symptom of business. Greeting unknown people with no intention of befriending is an alien concept to us. This is not how we were raised. As a child, we're taught to not talk to strangers since they're obviously kidnappers or worse. As a teen, we avoid strangers for suspicion that they're undercover narcs or nerds wanting to tag along. As an adult, we have come to the conclusion that if we don't already know these people, what's the point?

When strolling down a crowded sidewalk, you keep your eyes low. We consider it a breach of privacy for an uninvited person to make eye contact. Primitive tribes claim modern people steal their souls with cameras, but they're wrong. We pilfer souls with just our eyes. That's why nobody gets a look inside. We do our best to make sure nobody can make eye contact to greet us.

A majority of strangers saying hello want something from us. There's nothing random about their desire to look you straight in the eyes and make their presence known. When you're walking into a Las Vegas casino, the nice person saying hello is a timeshare salesperson ready to put the bite on you. Or they want to rent you a stripper for your hotel room. If you hear hello in a parking lot, you're about to get a sob story about being a few bucks short for a car part. The well-groomed person knocking on your door wants to say hello as if it's the key to getting you to swap religions. Or he has a mental illness and will latch onto you as his new best friend if you let him see your eyes. There's nothing casual about being greeted by a stranger. He always has an agenda. "Hello" is what a mosquito buzzes before sucking your blood.

You must overcome the phobia of greeting strangers to land the job of People Greeter. Are you capable of suppressing that gag reflex that makes you want to remain silent amongst unknown faces? Can you avoid blushing with shame when your job requires you to address strangers? If you can't greet people, you need to head back into the classifieds. Greeting is a majority of the job's duties. If you're unsure if you can handle the act of welcoming customers, let's find ways to test your abilities. Sometimes we need to bring these elements out of you. Practice makes perfect.

A Welcoming Welcome

For many applicants, the act of saying hello to complete strangers borders on a phobia. Often when people utter hello to a stranger, it's a defense mechanism. We feel threatened that this unknown person is approaching. The greeting serves as a way to throw them off their game for a second so that we can take appropriate measures to avoid attack. The hello makes them know that they've been identified and can't act as an invisible intruder. A greeting is the first motion in personal defense. A Walmart People Greeter's hello must never feel offensive or defensive. Your welcome must be welcoming. Can you be welcoming to others?

Before we go any further, go into the bathroom and turn on all the lights. Look at yourself in the mirror and say, "Welcome."

Do you feel welcomed by that person in the reflection? Can you sense warmth in your eyes and smile? Do you immediately say, "This person wants me here. He wants me to feel comfortable. He has my well-being at heart."

Or does your reflection make you sense an obligatory company policy being repeated to you? Are you being rushed to get through the door? Are you being judged in your stare? Is there coldness in your eyes that will repulse a sweet elderly lady who just wants a can of cat food for her precious Persian? You must be welcoming. Can you change your ways to become that person?

Before we focus on the way to properly greet people, let's address bad greeter role models. How do these bad greeters act to make a customer cringe upon entering the store? What can you learn from their uninviting ways?

The Stump

The Stump merely stands in the midst of the customer traffic uttering greetings as gasps. They barely respond when a customer comes up to him with a return item. Don't even think of asking The Stump where to find an item since he'll shrug towards the Customer Service desk. The Stump merely takes up space at the front of the store. A cardboard cutout of a NASCAR driver promoting a sponsor's product has a greater sense of pride in making customers feel at home. Once detected by management, stumps are swiftly removed from the high-profile greeter position.

The Robot

The Robot repeats, "Welcome to Walmart" in a constant monotone. His face is expressionless when meeting customers. If Walmart wanted an automaton as a greeter, they would have hired the Disney "Imagineers" to create a life-like substitute. The company wants to give customers the human experience. Don't allow your actions and tone to slip into a mechanical state. Allow customers to sense you are a real person.

The Chum King

The Chum King casually tosses a welcome while swiveling his head toward the incoming customers. He follows the rules laid out in public speaking classes. But there's no eye contact made with anyone entering. The Chum King casts his gaze on customers' foreheads. A few customers might believe they're been greeted, but a majority will sense they've been ignored. As a People Greeter, customers must know you're talking directly to them. A single greeting doesn't count for all the people in a ten-foot radius. Even though it sounds foreboding, your goal must be to insure that each customer receives direct eye contact and a warm welcome. When a family arrives, you are permitted to address them as a group. You don't have to give a welcome to each child squeezed into a shopping cart unless they're cute and responsive.

The Velvet Rope Guard

The Velvet Rope Guard blocks those he considers undesirable from entering with his attitude, tone and body language. He expects the customers to prove they're worthy to shop in his store. The Guard wants the customer to suck up to him. He reserves his greetings for beautiful people as if he were protecting the velvet rope outside a trendy nightclub. His stare shouts, "You better buy something big today if I deem you worthy to let you inside!" Walmart might have exclusive offers, but it does not want to exclude customers who aren't high rollers. This attitude will quickly get the Velvet Rope Guard shown the other side of the door.

Father of the Bride

The Father of the Bride acts as this is the happiest day of his life. He is overzealous with wide eyes and smiling open mouth. Customers who cross his path are treated like a long lost relative returning for a joyful event. He appears to be the verge of grabbing hands, bear hugging and two-cheek kissing customers. The hyper nature of his greeting may scare away people. He makes used car dealers look shy and reserved. The emotional outpouring of the Father of the Bride is too much for a person merely looking to buy a pack of hotdogs and a can of beans for their dinner. A greeter should be happy to see customers entering the store, but needs to remain calm and collected in his welcoming style. A simple rule is to act like a customer has shopped in a Walmart before.

The Buoy

The Buoy repeats his welcome whether or not anyone is within ten 10 feet. He is in a trance-like state with the greeting as a mantra. If he had a pair of tiny cymbals, he'd be ready for a religious cult. The Buoy is even worse than the Robot since he repeats the greeting without any prompting or concern. Even when the automatic doors swing open, the Buoy's stare is above the heads of incoming customers. It's almost an accident that the intended hear the greeting. This should not be confused as an elevated state of consciousness. The Buoy has become lost in the position. He only remembers his mission is to repeat the welcome.

He has no sense of why and how his greeting is to be delivered. In a harsh sense, he is having a mental meltdown. This behavior becomes his S.O.S. signal although most perceive him as being disrespectful. The truth is he can't handle the duties and can't cope with quitting the position. Everything inside him is shutting down to avoid the fear of what job can he lands next if he can't hack being a People Greeter. He has painted himself into a very dark corner and the only possible brightness reflects off a pink slip. The Buoy is about to be relieved of his scanner gun by an observant Customer Service Manager. You do not want to catch yourself falling into the Buoy's mindset since odds are high that you'll never psychically recover from the despair.

The Robert DeNiro Impersonator

The Robert DeNiro Impersonator upsets numerous customers with his tribute to America's finest actor. Rarely does a customer feel welcomed by *Taxi Driver*'s Travis Bickle saying, "You talkin' to me?" No one wants to overhear a soliloquy about a hard rain cleaning the scum out of the parking lot. Any of Jack La Motta's lines from *Raging Bull* are dismissible offenses with no first warning. Even though *Meet the Parents* is considered a comedy, there are few laughs when a customer fears he's encountered Jake Byrnes. A customer never wants to hear, "I will be watching you." This is not considered a polite greeting in any of the countries that have Walmart stores. DeNiro's "I'm watching you" hand gesture is never permitted even if a greeter suspects a shoplifter has entered. Your suspicions should be kept between you and the loss prevention team leader. If you need to role model yourself after a famous actor, think Jimmy Stewart or Tom Hanks. Pick an actor who didn't doesn't' scare your grandmother into making the sign of the cross when he appears on the TV screen. The final act of the Robert DeNiro Impersonator takes place in his elderly mother's basement as he pretends to still be a People Greeter like Rupert Pupkin in *The King of Comedy*.

Be Natural, Be You

What is left once you avoid patterning your technique after these bad examples? Hopefully, a cheerful and welcoming all-star greeter. There's not much effort that needs to be made to achieve this level of excellence. You don't need to spend years studying under the masters before you can feel secure in going solo.

Have a smile as your normal facial expression. Don't give a massive clown grin exposing teeth. Instead, maintain a slight upturn at the corners of your mouth. Look at the incoming customers in the eyes. Don't read their t-shirts since this might be perceived as staring at their chests. That's not a good way to greet anyone. Looking below a customer's nose is considered rude in parts of the world.

Welcome them with a positive greeting. Wait a second to see if they need any assistance with a return or directions to a department. If they are fine, move onto the next incoming customer. Don't ignore the 10-Foot Rule by spending 10 minutes on a customer who doesn't need help.

Now is the time for you to return to the mirror to see if you've improved your ability to be welcoming. You should see a marked improvement in yourself after reading about the bad examples of greeters and the simple steps needed to be good.

Did you feel welcomed this time? Did you exude warmth in greeting yourself? Were you ready to shop? Don't give up if you didn't feel completely welcomed by yourself. It might take a little time in front of that mirror. When you feel welcomed by yourself, then it's time to take the next step. How can you know if you have the skills, charm and stamina to be a professional welcomer? A greeter has to welcome more than the first customer of the day. Here are four scenarios for you to role-play in order to get a taste of the People Greeter experience. The scripts require a partner to play the customer while you assume the role of the Greeter. Do not swap off roles. You must master the welcoming skills of the People Greeter. This is serious business and not meant for entertainment purposes.

SCENARIO 1

```
Customer steps through the door.

GREETER: Welcome to Walmart.

Customer avoids making eye contact and walks
past the greeter.
```

SCENARIO 2

```
Customer steps through the door.

GREETER: Welcome to Walmart.

Customer barely nods and walks past the
greeter.
```

SCENARIO 3

Customer steps through the door.

GREETER: Welcome to Walmart.

CUSTOMER: Hi.

Customer walks past the Greeter.

SCENARIO 4

Customer steps through the door.

GREETER: Welcome to Walmart

CUSTOMER: I need to return these tube socks.

GREETER: Let me scan them first and then you can take them to Customer Service desk over there.

Greeter points to the customer service desk. Greeter uses the scanner gun on the UPC bar and puts sticker on the tube socks.

CUSTOMER: Thanks.

Customer walks past the Greeter.

Don't practice these scenarios once and call it a night. Your friend (or friends) must repeat the lines with you for two to three hours. No breaks. Does that sound like too much work? Are you already overwhelmed at the prospect of being that welcoming for so long? What do you think you're going to be doing during your shift? Practice prepares you for the reality of that first shift so you don't appear naive to your trainer.

Once you've mastered the role-playing, you'll need field training. It's easy to welcome a friend even if they're pretending to be someone else. Where can you get the experience of looking into the faces of strangers and welcome them? Do not wander down to Walmart and impersonate being a greeter with your own navy blue polo shirt and khaki pants. There is another place to see if you can handle the chore. Volunteer at your house of worship to greet people before the religious services. This is a perfect way to see how well you can welcome a large number of people at time. Think of this activity as an apprenticeship or playing in the minors before getting called up to start in the major leagues. You're working on your timing, your delivery, your stamina and your ability to look as good from the minute you walk on the floor as when you clock out. Besides never letting them see you sweat, you need to never let them see you lose your welcoming disposition.

Nobody needs to think you didn't care they came to Walmart instead of a competitor. If you need a reason to be happy towards them: remember that without customers at your Walmart, they'll shutdown the store. This means you'll be back on the job hunt. You ready for the mental pain and harsh rejection? Now do you understand why you're really happy to see the customers walk through the front doors?

Once you've mastered hello, be prepared to also say goodbye in your role as a greeter. The farewell doesn't take precedence over a greeting. But it's a nice touch if you have time for a departing customer. Let them know that you want them to return soon. The goodbye can be just a simple, "Thanks for coming by." You don't need to ask them if they found everything they were looking for since that should be the responsibility of a cashier. Do not restrict your goodbyes for customers with a full cart of purchases. This time they might have only bought a candy bar, but the customer might purchase an expensive high definition television on their next visit. If you ignore them, they might take their business elsewhere. Your welcome and goodbye makes an impression and reflects in sales.

You aren't obligated to always say, "Welcome to Walmart." People Greeters are known for asking, "Hello, how are you doing?" But why do you even want to make it sound like you're interested in starting a conversation? The goal is to welcome people and not go through their recent medical history and personal problems. There are customers eager to unload detailed descriptions so don't tempt them. You won't find yourself being tongue tied by sticking with the simple "Welcome to Walmart" greeting.

Welcome the World

Walmart is a global enterprise with an international clientele. People around the world know of Walmart and seek it out when they visit the United States of America. New immigrants feel comfortable in the store. There are days when you'll feel like an employee of the United Nations. In case you want to spice up your welcome when you know the nationality or heritage of a regular customer, here's a glossary for how to say welcome in various countries and languages:

Albana - *Mire se vini*

Arabic - *Ahlan Wa Sahlan*

Aruban(Dutch Caribbean) - *Bon Bini* (Bong Be-knee)

Australian - *Cooee Cobber* or *G'day Mate*

Burmese - *Kyo-so-ba-thi*

Catalonian - *Benvinguts*

Chechen - *Marsha dogheela*

Chinese - *Huanying guanglin* or *Huan ying*

Cyprus - *Kalosorisate*

Czech - *Vitame Vas* or *Vitejte*

Danish - *Velkommen*

Dutch - *Welkom*

Esperanto - *Bonvenon*

Estonian - *Teretulemast*

Finnish: *Tervetuloa*

Ewe - *Woezor* (pronounced Wozen)

Flemish - *Welkom*

French - *Bienvenue*

Frisian - *Wolkom*

Gaelic - *Failte*

German - *Willkommen*

Ghana - *Akwaaba*

Greek - *Kalos ilthes*

Hawaiian - *E komo mai* (pronounced "eh como my")

Hebrew - *Baruch haba*

Hindi - *Swaa-gat hai*

Indonesian - *Selamat Datang*

Irish - *Cead Mile Failte* and *Failte romhat*

Italian - *Benvenuto*

Japanese - *Irasshaimase*

Korean - *Oh so, Osay-o*

Malaysia - *Selamat Datang*

Maltese - *Merhba*

Netherlands - *Welkom*

New Zealand - *Kia Ora* (pronounced "Key or ra")

Norwegian - *Velkommen*

Persian - *Khosh amadid*

Polish - *Dzień dobry* and *Serdecznie witamy*!

Portuguese - *Bem Vinda* and *Bem Vindo*

Romania - *Multumesc*

Russian - *Dobro pozhalovat*

Slovenian - *Dobrodosli*

Spanish - *Bienvenido*

Swiss German - *Greuzi* (pronounced "GREW-tzih")

Swedish - *Valkommen*

Tagalog - *Mabuhay*

Tamil - *Vanga*

Tibetan - *Tashi Delek*

Ukraine - *Laskavo prosymo*

Southern United States - *Howdy*

Urdu - *Khosh amadid* and *Tash-reef Laa-i-ye*

Uzbekistan - *Hush kelibsiz*

Vietnamese - Kinh Chao Quy Khach

Welsh - *Croeso cynnes*

Wales - *Croeso* (pronounced "Croysso")

Yugoslavian - *Dobrodosli*

Please take note that these welcomes from around the globe were copied from a collection of placemats handed out a family-style restaurant in Butte, Montana. The translations might not be reliable. Although none of the words appear to be obscene in their native tongues. It would be best to let the foreign language speaker know you're a novice linguist and not ex-interpreter for the United Nations.

The only person who says hello to strangers more than a People Greeter is a candidate for the presidency of the United States during the early primaries. Once the nominations are locked up, the presidential hopeful no longer has to say hello anyone who wanders into a rally. Their greetings are reserved for major donors and political machine operators.

Once you lock down the People Greeter position, nothing slows down. The nice part of your job is you're not responsible for kissing babies, which is good. You're going to have enough issues with communicable diseases without coming in constant contact with small children. They are petri dishes of germs. You might want to keep a small bottle of antibacterial hand sanitizer in your pocket for encounters with sickly customers of all ages. This doesn't make you a germophobe unless you squirt your hands after every customer penetrates your 10-foot perimeter.

Another item to keep in your pocket to help you be more welcoming is a container of breath mints. No matter how good you think your breath is, it changes during the workday. The change is never for the best. Every hour or so, you will need to freshen your breath. Halitosis will not make you welcoming. The good news is that you can always buy more breath fresheners and mints during your breaks. They sell a wide variety at Walmart. Choose a mild mint. You don't want to overwhelm the customers with a harsh odor that could be more repulsive than your worst breath.

A Walmart Greeter must be as welcoming in words, attitude and odor. He can't allow his ability to welcome a person wane over the course of hours. This is an important position. Can you say those three magic words to turn a customer into an invited guest? Are you ready to tell a stranger, "Welcome to Walmart?" And then repeat that welcome for the next thousand strangers over the course of your shift? If yes, you need to welcome yourself to Walmart first.

POP QUIZ

1) What's the prime job of a Walmart People Greeter?

    A. Don't block the security cam.

    B. Make everyone knows their job.

    C. Announce the latest price markdowns.

    D. Greet People.

2) Where should you look when welcoming a customer?

    A. The customer's t-shirt.

    B. Your shoes.

    C. The exit sign.

    D. The customer's eyes.

3) A People Greeter should welcome:

    A. Every customer.

    B. Regular customers.

    C. Rich customers.

    D. First time customers.

4) What Robert DeNiro impersonation works best with customers?

    A. Travis Bickle in *Taxi Driver*.

    B. Jack Byrnes in *Meet the Parents*.

    C. Jake LaMotta in Raging Bull.

    D. Never ever impersonate Robert DeNiro.

5) Why should you use a breath mint?

    A. Cover up your liquid lunch.

    B. Avoid offending customers.

    C. Smell like Wintergreen Forest

    D. Promote the latest breath freshener.

6) Which Greeter do you wish to model yourself after?

    A. The Robot.

    B. The Buoy.

    C. The Stump.

    D. None of the above.

Write down "Welcome" in as many different languages as you can remember without peeking.

_____

_____

The Seven Secrets of Great Walmart People Greeters

ANSWER KEY

1) **D**. - Walmart People Greeters greet people. If you haven't gotten that concept from the title of the job, you need to start re-reading the book now.

2) **D** - Eye contact is a major part of your welcoming the customer. This is the way they know you are greeting them and not just tossing out your words to everyone in the immediate vicinity.

3) **A**. - Every customer deserves a "Welcome to Walmart." Even if you remember them from previous trips, you need to welcome them again. You must welcome people no matter how much money you suspect they'll spend in the store.

4) **D**. - Never ever impersonate Robert DeNiro while in your official position. If you were that great at DeNiro, you'd be a cast member on *Saturday Night Live* and not wearing navy blue and khaki.

5) **B**. - Nobody likes smelling bad breath.

6) **D**. - All of the named examples are bad examples.

7) That's nice, but being multilingual is not required for the position.

SECRET THREE: BE A FACE

Walmart is a faceless corporation. What living person do you think of when Walmart is mentioned? Can you name anyone who appears in its advertising? Ask a friend what living person comes to mind when they think of Walmart? Odds are high that the face they imagine isn't a match with yours.

There's no corporate owner staking his reputation in advertisement campaigns. Walmart doesn't hire celebrity spokespeople to pitch sales. An energetic cartoon character doesn't dominate its commercials. At one point there was a smiley face that promoted its "Rolling Back Prices" slogan. The smiley face lacked personality. He was merely happy, yellow and knocking down prices. He was no Trix Rabbit or Chester Cheeto. Kids didn't embrace him as anything more than the ubiquitous yellow smiley face that's been around for decades. The smiley face has been replaced on the latest Walmart logo by what is either a digital sun or a computer's "on" button. Either way, it's not a face since the symbol doesn't have eyes.

Decades ago there was a face. Founder Sam Walton was an icon for Walmart as the stores spread across the country and around the world. He sold his idea of what a discount store could mean to America. He tirelessly promoted his chain as an effective alternative to Sears. He had no problem being the face of the store that contained his name. When he died in 1992, his public presence faded. He wasn't transformed into a commercial corporate identity like Disney did with Walt Disney or KFC did with Colonel Sanders. His philosophies guide the corporate headquarters in Bentonville, Arkansas although his identity has lost prominence in the minds of consumers. The average Sam's Club member doesn't know he's "the Sam." They consider Sam a made up name like Mrs. Butterworth, Betty Crocker or Victoria of Victoria's Secret. Sam sounds like a name conceived by a marketing firm to reflect a customer who prefers to buy in bulk at reduced prices. Sam was a man and not a marketing creation.

The lack of a familiar human spokesperson has allowed consumers to view Walmart as an edifice. They believe computers intent on creating an efficient sales machine without factoring the human cost control the corporation. The perception is that numbers control the executives and not their hearts. This translates into a consumer sensing nothing human or emotional about his Walmart shopping experience. To him, Walmart is a joyless, gigantic vending machine.

Who can put a human face on his Walmart shopping experience? You can. Yes, you! You can be the face people think of when they shop at Walmart.

Your welcoming smile as a People Greeter restores a sense of humanity to a customer's misconception. Your delightful disposition assures that customer that the store is not a soulless behemoth. He is not stepping into a vast warehouse of products that have been systematically organized to get him to buy more than what is on his shopping list. He enters *your* store. Your face reflects a sense of pride at what's offered inside.

Check Your Ego at the Door

But don't act like you own the place. You don't want the manager getting upset at you putting on airs. Ownership is not your role. You're the host of the greatest shopping experience on Earth. To thousands of customers, your face reminds them that people work at Walmart and not robots.

Are there people you'd rather not show your face around? Would you hide your face by ducking behind a display of soft drinks if these acquaintances walked through the doors? Would you feel a sense of utter shame if they knew you were working as People Greeter? Who are they? Friends? Family members? Former co-workers? Old bosses? High school enemies? The third-grade teacher who swore you'd never be a success with your attitude? Write down a list of people who can't see you in navy blue and khaki. Next to each name; explain why his or her judgment of you is worth more than putting food on your table. How can those people embarrass you so much that you'd rather lose a paycheck than feel their disapproval? What puts them above you? How can they stand in judgment of you working at Walmart when they're shopping in *your* store? Can they really turn their noses upward and continue to sniff out the latest deals and bargain prices?

What good are they as friends and family members if they don't understand the predicament that led to this position in life? You don't want their pity or charity. If it was about pity and charity, you would have hit them up for cash or favors earlier. They just need to understand that this is a better alternative than having you couch surf until you win the lottery or die. It's guaranteed that your old high school enemy will mock you for saying, "Welcome to Walmart." But he'd find a reason to trash your life if you were driving a solid gold car and blowing your nose with $100 bills. You're never going to change the attitude of a devoted jerk. You no longer work for your ex-boss. He doesn't matter in your life. In today's economic situation, your ex-boss might also be an ex-employee of your ex-company. He'll leave the store empty handed since he'll be too embarrassed to apply for a People Greeter position and work under *you*. Odds are high that by now your third-grade teacher is dead. So her arrival will never be an issue.

This isn't the most embarrassing job you can ever have. Here are a few occupations that should make you feel shame: Overnight janitor at an adult bookstore, rodeo clown at a nudist ranch, junk bond king and cocktail waitress at a cockfighting ring. Doesn't being a People Greeter sound like a noble calling compared to those positions? You have no need to hide your face when standing near the entrance.

Be the Best You, You Can Be

The best part of being the face of Walmart is that you can be yourself. No longer are you required to spend hours in front the mirror shaving the years off your appearance with tweezers and hair dye. Forget wasting hours at a spa getting your face so tight that your well-earned wrinkles get yanked flat. Skip spending outrageous dollars at the trendy clothing store to not stick out at meetings with last year's wardrobe. You shall no longer have to pour money into the false fountains of youth. You don't have to fake that you're barely out of college when you interview for the position. Older applicants are welcomed during the People Greeter hiring process. How long has it been since you resembled your age while on the clock?

Nobody wants to grow old while at a corporation. The personal choice of aging is heavily discouraged in our society. Looking old is considered an impediment to being a useful part of the workforce. Companies crave youth since it resembles a futuristic outlook that adapts well to an always-changing marketplace. Old employees are marked as "traditionalists" that weigh things down with their desire to remain in the past. They are bound by the historic methods from their bygone era. Their ideas are dismissed as serious contenders with the old truism, "You can't teach an old dog new tricks." How many times did you hear this as the reason for a longtime co-worker being escorted out of the building? People who look old are viewed as having a fear of computers, smartphones, tablets and FM radio. Old employees ought to ride a horse drawn buggy into the parking lot since they're Amish in the eyes of the youngsters down the hall. Young employees rarely ask advice from older employees for the fear that the codger's epic answer will blather about how things were done back in the 20th century. History is as useful as a crutch in a 100 meter dash. You must refrain from exposing your true experiences and hair color to be taken seriously.

A touch of grey marks you for elimination. You're no longer considered a young gun. There's a target on your back when your age shows. The latest fresh out of college hire marks you in his crosshairs. Even though they're young rebels, they use the traditional ammo to character assassinate those considered hobbled by time. Their whispers circulate that the older employee thinks "inside the box." Experience only makes you out of touch with modern needs. Veteran employees are merely counting the days to cashing in their 401Ks. They can't see the future beyond a lush retirement community in Florida. The seniors are deadweight keeping the company from soaring unencumbered to its natural heights. This mindset is nothing new. This how lions devour each other in the pride. Survival of the fittest also applies to the corporate jungle. Decades ago, you sized up the previous generation's dinosaurs who couldn't comprehend a touchtone phone. Seniority has always been perceived as weak rungs in the corporate ladder that a newbie hire plans to climb in record time. Everybody craves to be the youngest CEO at a corporation with a dashing portrait hanging in the executive dining hall. No one has time to wait his turn. What's the point of being on top after thirty years on the clock? Where's the fun in that? Showing your true age represents a concession that the youthful dream is dead.

But for a People Greeter age is a positive characteristic and not a weakness. There's no secret mandate to hire young and sexy for the position. Hundred year old People Greeters celebrate their milestone birthdays at the store entrance. A centenarian is not focused on looking 20 when checking his appearance in the employee bathroom. This position allows you to embrace your face. There's no burden of looking hip, modern and cool in your sleek new haircut. You may look the way you want to look and not how you're expected to be groomed to keep up with the new school. Finally you are free to grow a mustache or curl your hair into a '70s style perm.

Don't take this message wrong. Your appearance can't go to seed. You still need to be well groomed before punching the clock. Hygiene is important. They're not hiring hobos and hillbillies.

Passive Security

Why would a company want older employees in a high-profile position? This squashes the trend of mall stores that hire young and sexy college kids to tempt customers inside. Why would the largest retailer in the world go against the youth tide? Having the incoming customers look into the face of an older employee is part of a passive security plan for dissuading shoplifters. Would you steal from grandma or grandpa? A normal person feels disgust when reading a news article about a senior citizen being the victim of crime. How can someone be so cruel to the elderly? The mature face of a People Greeter should flash in the consciousness of a would-be shoplifter before he pockets an item. Of course, this guilt-laden crime-prevention plan fails if the culprits hate their grandparents.

Dress Code

While you can be free to express your face, this liberty doesn't extend to your wardrobe. For the longest time employees of Walmart merely wore a blue company smock over their clothes. The back of the smock contained the friendly question of "How may I help you?" The smock made them instantly identifiable by customers. Previously People Greeters picked out clothing that expressed their personality and didn't clash with the blue smock. Their fashion selections helped them be a face and body for the store. Over the last few years, Walmarts across America dropped the smock to institute a dress code. As far as dress codes go, it's not too harsh. Employees must wear a navy blue polo-style shirt and khaki pants. There are plenty of choices within the guidelines. There are twenty different shades of khaki. Not to mention hundreds of brands with different cuts. You should be able to find a pair of khaki pants that appeal to you. The same is true with the shirts you'll wear. This isn't like you're being asked to dress in corporate uniform or a clown costume. Every day will forevermore be business casual.

Maybe you're a rebel who refuses to dress as you're told. You demand to express your individuality no matter what the circumstances. You stopped being told what to wear when you moved out of your parents' house. What are you really protesting? Why waste your time locating the Walmart in your area that still uses the blue smocks? And what's going to prevent them from adopting the dress code a few weeks after you land the job? The dress code is there for your emotional well-being.

How can a dress code be mentally good for you? Do you really want to wear your old business clothes to the new job? Imagine catching your reflection in the mirror during a shift. Beneath the blue smock is that expensive shirt and slacks you wore to your old job. Are you ready to be reminded of your time behind a comfy desk with a receptionist filtering your calls? After that memory, how are you going to smile and say, "Welcome to Walmart?" The weight of your past clings to the fabric of your old wardrobe like pine sap. You don't want to waste your paycheck on therapy. The dress code keeps you from thinking so much about things that you had no control over. It also saves time. For decades you spent an hour picking out the workday's wardrobe so you'd look just right for the office. You'd deliberate if the necktie tied the shirt and the jacket together. The dress code eliminates such nonsense. If you buy five sets of navy blue shirts and khaki pants, you've eliminated all that frustration of coordinating an outfit. Grab a shirt and a pair of pants and you're done. Why waste your time coordinating and accessorizing? You're getting older and your remaining time needs to be spent on better things. This will be the first positive step to simplifying your life. Brain activity will be at a minimum when you get dressed. This will help in the early days as you come to accept the job. You won't get frustrated and accidentally give a sour face to customers. The only thing you'll have to think about is that when all the navy blue shirts and khaki pants are in the laundry hamper, your work week is over.

Another positive feature of the dress code is the inability of customers to recognize you when you're off duty. Regular customers might believe you're any other person if you're wearing anything that's not navy blue and khaki. When you shop at a different store, you won't have to worry about them asking how Walmart prices compare. You don't need to work off the clock. It's like when a superhero takes off his cape and insignia jersey so he can eat lunch in peace. When it's time to be the face of Walmart, you put on the navy blue and khaki and greet away.

Don't be embarrassed to put your face on the internet. There are quite a few People Greeters that have a presence on social media sites. A greeter named Smitty at the store in Sedalia, Missouri has his own Facebook fan page. Nearly 16,000 people have "liked" him. That's a sold out arena for a rock star. People from around the world have become fans of a man who says, "Welcome to Walmart" in the heartland. Smitty's celebrity status was featured in *Walmart World Magazine*. This certifies how the company doesn't mind positive publicity. Being positive is the most important thing about your internet connections. Don't post anything that's controversial. Don't use the site to speak badly of supervisors or settle scores with co-workers. Don't grouse about anything corporate related. This is a quick way to get fired. Don't post pictures of customers with snide comments about their actions or looks. Avoid topics that can upset customers. Don't take sides when it comes to sports teams, politics and religion. The best thing to do is state the obvious. Mention how spring is coming and customers might want to visit the garden store. Remind people they need to stock up on potato chips for the big game. Don't quote sale prices because you might be wrong and you'll get in trouble. A few lessons you can learn from Smitty is to avoid using your last name. Frequently check the site to remove any nasty comments that might be construed as anti-Walmart. Never update your page while on the clock. Management will notice if you're using your phone for internet postings. While the site might be about the store, it's not considered company business. If you follow these rules, you'll be a worldwide face for your local store just like Smitty.

The people who will consistently view you as the face of Walmart are the kids. Many of the stores supply the People Greeters with stickers to pass out. The kids will swear you run the show since you hand out the treats. The round smiley face stickers are gold to elementary school students. Little kids will make you feel like their retail granddad as they beg for another sticker.

Walmart doesn't need another hero

The place your face should never appear is the front page of a newspaper as a hero for disarming a violent criminal. A major rule of the People Greeter is "Don't Be a Hero." You're considered part of loss prevention, but only as minor assistance in the greater operation. You're not there to act as a security guard or rent-a-cop.

When a customer sets off the security gate alarm; you ask them to stop, show a receipt and check his bag or cart to make sure things match. A majority of the time, the alarm went off because a cashier forgot to deactivate a security tag. If this is the case, you apologize for the inconvenience, hand back his purchases and wave goodbye as the customer heads toward the parking lot. That is the best case scenario involving an innocent customer.

There are worse case scenarios and you must be prepared for them. Many shoplifters are repeat offenders and don't want to get caught. They won't let themselves get tripped up and detained by a People Greeter. When you ask someone to show you his receipt make sure you're not backed into a corner and have over an arm's length between you and the suspect. This space is for your security. An experienced shoplifter will charge you when he feels threatened. It's like dealing with a wild animal. If you sense he is lunging, back off and alert your asset protection coordinator. Don't feel the necessity to physically challenge the suspect. You're not being a coward if you back away. You might have been a decorated war hero in Korea, Vietnam or any other conflict. You might have been an all-state football champion in high school. You might have wrestled bears as a summer job to pay your college tuition. But those days are behind you. Your body can't handle the punishment it absorbed in your younger days. You ache enough without taking a punch in the face from a punk kid.

There are plenty of reports involving shoplifters assaulting elderly People Greeters. They don't care about your age or grandchildren.

They want to punch you and run out the doors. The face of Walmart cannot afford to have a black eye.

Don't chase after a criminal who's run out of the store. Once again, you're in no shape to race across the parking lot. There's a chance you might have a heart attack. Don't physically exert yourself in any way. Let the younger loss prevention or asset protection employees handle that stuff. Nobody should be getting on your case because you let one get away. You weren't hired to be muscle. The main thing you need to do in a shoplifting situation is avoid blocking the security cameras from getting a good view of the culprit. Your face should not dominate the video footage.

In an extreme case, a shoplifter might pull out a gun. Get out of the way at that moment. Corporate policy AP-09 demands you disengage and withdraw if a weapon is exposed. You might think you're going to be a hero by disarming them. Don't sneak up on them and use a karate move you remembered from an action film. Shoplifters want to escape and not kill anyone. Give the culprit a free passage to an exit and let the police handle it.

There are major consequences if your hero moment fails.

What if your struggle leads to the gun going off? A bullet might hit an innocent customer. This will lead to a major lawsuit. Even if you are the only one injured in the struggle, there's still a trip to the emergency room. Do you know how much the shoplifter would have to steal in order to equal the cost of treating a bullet wound? He'd have to drive off with all of the high definition TVs on display. Walmart doesn't turn a profit if it's paying a fortune in medical costs.

The penalty for breaking Policy AP-09 is immediate dismissal. In one well-known incident six employees had detained a shoplifter in the loss prevention room,. The shoplifter pulled out a gun and declared he was leaving before the police arrived. One employee hid, another called the police while the remaining four jumped the gunman and disarmed him. While no one was injured, the four heroes found themselves unemployed. The two that followed policy are still working. Are newspaper heroics worth your job?

Nobody becomes a Walmart People Greeter to embrace a life of danger.

Just Rewards

The sweetest compliment you'll ever receive is when a customer asks if you've been on vacation because she hasn't haven't seen you in a while. You don't know this person, but your smile has had an impact on her. That means you are the face of Walmart to her.

POP QUIZ

1) What living person is the face of Walmart?

_____

2) What does the new logo for Walmart look like?

    A. A digital sun.

    B. An "on" button.

    C. I'm not a modern art critic.

    D. A smiley face.

3) Who is the "Sam" in Sam's Club?

    A. Any Sam who buys in bulk.

    B. Sam I Am.

    C. Sam Wich.

    D. Sam Walton

4) Who is the next face of Walmart?

    A. A future beauty queen.

    B. A country star.

    C. A TV star.

    D. You.

5) As a People Greeter, you remind customers that Walmart is:

   A. A soulless edifice

   B. A vending machine

   C. Run by people that care

   D. The first signs that the robots are taking over.

6) List the people you don't want to see your face at Walmart:

_____

_____

7) Explain why you'd rather starve instead of letting the people in the previous answer see you as a People Greeter.

_____

_____

8) What color must your slacks be under the Walmart dress code?

   A. Khaki.

   B. Cranberry.

   C. Kiwi.

   D. Black Watch Plaid.

9) What style shirt must you wear as a People Greeter?

    A. Tanktop.

    B. Softball Jersey.

    C. Polo-style

    D. Turtleneck.

10) Who is Smitty?

    A. A notorious shoplifter.

    B. Corporate policy AP-09's nickname.

    C. The name of Walmart's Smiley Face character.

    D. An internet famous Walmart People Greeter.

11) Corporate policy AP-09 addresses:

    A. Lunch breaks

    B. Bathroom clean up

    C. Dogs in the store

    D. What do when a shoplifter has a weapon.

The Seven Secrets of Great Walmart People Greeters

ANSWER KEY

1) No living person is the face of Walmart. This is why you can easily be the face of Walmart to the thousands of customers that enter your store.

2) **C**. - You might have to go to an expensive art college to figure out what this logo is supposed to be.

3) **D**. - Sam Walton was a real man. He put the "Wal" part of-"Wal"mart. He's the "Sam" in "Sam's" Club. He's not a fictional character created by a marketing firm like Ronald McDonald.

4) **D**. - Have you not paid attention to this secret? It's all about you getting to be the face of Walmart.

5) **C**. - Your face brings a human quality to the corporation. You make sure people don't think they're dealing with a vending machine run by robots.

6) Nobody should be on this list. How dare they judge you?

7) No one should ever make you starve so that you can live up to his standards. The only exception should be if you're a supermodel about to lose a multi-million dollar endorsement deal.

8) **A**. - Tan.

9) **C**. - You don't have to also buy a polo pony when you purchase the shirt.

10) **D**. - You may want to look up Smitty on the internet to see how he deals with his celebrity status.

11) **D**. - This policy reminds you that you're not supposed to be a hero as a People Greeter. Don't risk your life to prevent someone from stealing a toaster oven.

SECRET FOUR: KNOW YOUR STORE

Entering a Walmart can be an overwhelming experience to a novice customer used to smaller stores. Even a veteran shopper can be stunned by the enormity and unlimited vastness of what's offered under one roof. How huge can a Walmart get? There are shopping malls smaller than a Walmart.

The average Walmart Supercenter is 200,000 square feet. The best way to put that into perspective is to imagine four football fields stuffed inside a single building. Nearly a million items are spread throughout the floorspace on racks, shelves and displays. This is the 8th Wonder of the Consumer World. Nearly everything a person needs from birth to death is stocked.

Customer Service can order cradles and caskets through the company's website. Under a single roof is a department store, a pharmacy, a grocery store, a car care center, a one hour photo and a garden center. They can contain fast food restaurants, banks, hair stylists, nail salons, optical centers, cellphone shops, photography studios and sometimes a gas station in the parking lot. It's a mall unto itself. What Walmart doesn't stock, you don't really need in your life.

People can be on the verge of a panic attack when stepping inside. They might only want to buy a single tomato or a box of diapers. Right when those automatic doors open, they'll regret not going to a convenience store and paying more to be faced with less. A phobia takes over their thought process. They fear being trapped like a mice in a cheese-less gondola maze or stumbling across a seething minotaur in the center of the clothing rack labyrinth. They're paralyzed with the fear of an avalanche of hundreds of soda bottles trapping them. No one will be able to find them in the remote aisle. They'll never see their loved ones again. They're frightened that they may never leave the store alive. How can there be a safe passage to what they need? Why are they risking their lives for the sake of an ironing board? The frightened customer doesn't know where Walmart stocks the ironing boards? Can it be in small appliances? Maybe it's with laundry detergent? Maybe it's in home furnishings? How about industrial cleaning supplies? Can there be a section dedicated to ironing boards? They've never looked for an ironing board since it's something rarely purchased more than once in a lifetime. Their confusion is overwhelming.

Your friendly face is the only thing keeping them from collapsing in a fetal position and hyperventilating. Your greeting is a beacon of hope that keeps them from turning around and screaming as they run into the parking lot. You remind them that they're not alone when entering the imposing aisles packed with millions of items that aren't on their list. Everything they want might be inside the store, but what are the odds of them being easily found? They can't afford to be the victim of a fruitless expedition. They don't have time to run around the store looking for the item or chasing after phantom sales clerks for assistance. They know help will be there right when they step in the store. The People Greeter can give them directions to pinpoint what's on their shopping list. The People Greeter must exude the attitude of compassionate authority. Are you ready to give them an answer that will calm their fears? Or will you choose to compound their anxieties and dread?

What's the worst thing you can say to a customer wanting to know where you stock an item? Think hard. Reverse the situation to when you're the shopper. What don't you want to be told by a store employee when you can't find a specific product? What makes you think they hired a clueless moron that has no pride in their store? "We don't have it," is not the worst answer. There's nothing disheartening at being told they're out of stock or don't carry it. At least you're getting a prompt answer. The most frustrating thing you can tell someone is, "I'm not sure. You need to ask customer service." They've just entered the store and now they're trapped in a line with an empty cart. They don't want the drama of being stuck behind a person attempting to return a bag full of clothes without a receipt. This is a form of torture for an already anxious shopper. The next time you see this customer, they'll be rushing out the doors with empty hands and a promise to never step inside your store.

Why should a shopper think they can navigate the store if the People Greeter hasn't an idea where to locate a simple item? Sending them to customer service is reinforcing the fear that things are randomly scattered around the floor. This is not a yardsale or a flea market. The trucks don't arrive from the warehouse and boxes tossed in the nearest empty space. The floor plan isn't the aftermath of a tornado zipping down the aisles. There is order. An employee's ignorance of that order sends the message that there's no way for a regular person to comprehend the shelves. Don't give them the fear that beyond you exists a vast wilderness haunted by a monster who consumes consumers. You are a People Greeter and not a People Scarer.

How can you calm down a customer on the verge of a panic attack? The first thing is to never be the employee that frustrates you as a customer. You despise a sales clerk who gives you a shrug as if it's your problem that you can't find the non-dairy creamer. Never let them be your role model or excuse for bad etiquette. Establish yourself as an ideal. Pledge that you'll never answer any question with a shrug. You must make it your business to answer with words so that a customer will never regret thinking you can help. A compassionate authoritative attitude calms the customer so you can understand what they need. You must give a real answer that reassures them that it's not that complicated of a store. Don't look annoyed and point them towards customer service as a form of punishment. Make it your business to know what's behind you and where it is.

Don't be overwhelmed with the task of memorizing everything stocked on the shelves. You don't need to know if the store stocks the 10 ounce, 12 ounce or 16 ounce cans of ten different varieties of baked beans. You don't have to know every flavor of ice cream in the freezer section. There's no necessity to memorize how many bolts of fabric are available. But you do need to know if your store has a fabric department.

The best way to take stock of the shelves is to shop. Don't merely skip to your favorite sections and head to the cashier. You aren't shopping for yourself anymore. Grab a shopping cart and slowly proceed down every aisle. Pay attention to what is on the shelves. Look high and low as you wheel your cart around. Nothing can be dismissed as unworthy of your attention. Don't skip a section because it doesn't interest you or have importance on your life. You might not have kids, but you better visit the baby section. Don't skip the pet department because you're allergic to cats. Riding the bus doesn't excuse you from having knowledge about auto care products. Being a man doesn't forbid you from locating the feminine hygiene products and being a woman is no rationale for skipping the boxer shorts section. Does it seem too big of an effort to walk this much? Maybe you need to save your time and energy for sitting by the phone thinking your old boss is calling to let you know they made a big mistake? Was that too harsh of a reality slap? You can always use the exercise to maintain an active body. Pushing a cart around Walmart is good for your heart.

When you complete walking the entire store; go home and draw the layout of the store with the various departments identified. A few hours later, return to the store and see how your map matches the actual layout. Feel free to make corrections. When you're done shopping, return to your kitchen table and draw a fresh map after the verification visit. Now match it up with your answer key. How close are you getting to knowing each section? Keep up this study process until you have a clue how each section flows into the next.

Where Is It?

When you feel secure in the layout of the store, it's time to take things to the next step: Give directions on how to find items. This is a communications skill that may take a little time to master. Don't get frustrated if it takes a while to exhibit effortless talent in giving directions. You practice and learn from your mistakes when it doesn't count against you. Perfect your directions now so you'll look like a pro on the first day you proudly stand at the People Greeter station.

The directions should be the shortest and most concise that you can possible give. Don't turn into the yokel at the gas station that gives fifteen twists and turns with a shortcut that involve climbing over an open freezer full of crab claws until you dead end them with a "you can't quite get there from here" disclaimer. The customer isn't wanting directions to get to your favorite "tourist-free" vacation getaway. They have enough tension thinking about their shopping lists and dreading getting lost amongst the countless aisles. Keep your answer extremely simple.

The best technique is to reduce your answer to four directions. The four turns might not involve the shortest route, but it's the safest for them to understand. You can always preface your answer by saying, "This is a little bit longer, but it's the easiest way." Can you keep things down to only four directions?

The most asked question you'll hear should be the easiest. "Where's the bathroom?" You need to have that down. You need to be able to give that direction and any store policies about what's allowed in the bathroom without thinking. Can you tell me how to get to the bathroom in four directions?

1. _____

2. _____

3. _____

4. _____

On your next visit to Walmart, follow your directions to see where they lead. Did you successfully direct me to the bathroom sign or will you have to order a cleanup in the hardware department? Can you refine these directions even more?

The second most asked question is "Where's the pharmacy?" You have to be careful on this one because the person asking the question is either sick or getting the medicine for a loved one who doesn't want to wait long for their precious medicine. How would you direct a customer to the Pharmacy counter?

1. _____

2. _____

3. _____

4. _____

While your store might have a clearly marked Pharmacy near the entrance, a customer might be too overwhelmed to notice the obvious signs. Never give the customer the sense that they're blind. Let them chuckle at the fact that they can't notice something so obvious. If they say anything self-deprecating about not seeing something so visible, merely smile so they know it's not that unusual. Do not contribute to the conversation since you might end up touching a sore topic with them. Once they know where to go; you need to get them on their way. There are more customers coming through the doors with questions for you.

Many of the store's customers are Spanish language speakers. Don't panic if you aren't bilingual. You don't need to run out to a language school to become conversational with them. This is not a necessity for the job although it might serve you well if you're curious about learning a second language. Ultimately there are only two words in Spanish you need to know. When they ask for "*el Baño,*" they want to go to the bathroom. If they ask for "*la farmacía,*" they want to be pointed toward the pharmacy. If they ask for something that completely confuses you, show them to customer service so they can locate an associate or manager who speaks their language. Don't feel like you've failed as a People Greeter because you're not a translator at the United Nations. You will want to feel bad if you can't direct an English speaking person to the right shelf.

Now it's time to test yourself with a five popular items that customers always end up needing in an emergency. What's the best path from the entrance of your nearby Walmart? Don't cheat by looking at your old store maps. You might want to use pencil unless you want to buy another copy of this book.

Milk

1. _____

2. _____

3. _____

4. _____

Duct Tape

1. _____

2. _____

3. _____

4. _____

Diapers

1. _____

2. _____

3. _____

4. _____

Sudafed

1. _____

2. _____

3. _____

4. _____

Beer

1. _____

2. _____

3. _____

4. _____

Take a friend to Walmart, give them your directions to the five items and see if they can locate the products. You may observe them navigate the store, but under no circumstances can you interfere. Don't even hint with a head point if you've sent them into the women's fashions looking for duct tape. You're only going to cheat yourself if you can't recognize and improve your errors. Take notice as to ways you can refine your directions. Nobody is grading you. This will not go down in your permanent record or as part of your job interview. Although your friend will probably humiliate you on the drive home for sending him into the plastic flowers section for diapers. If he's really your friend, he'll be rooting for you to get it right. Make sure you treat him to lunch at whatever fast food franchise is inside the Walmart.

How would you describe your first attempt at giving directions? Did your friend have five items in their cart without any issues? Or would he complain to the store manager about hiring an incompetent worker? Luckily he's your friend and not your first customer so there's no repercussions. There's just the knowledge of what you need to improve your skills.

When you're ready to try it again, bring a different friend to Walmart and give him fresh directions to the five items. Did his shopping trip go smoother than then your first friend? Are you feeling more secure about how to guide someone around the aisles to the right shelf? Ready for the next challenge? Bring your original friend to store to see if he can find these more esoteric items with only your help. While you might be panicked by the list, remember that you've spent so much time in the store going through the aisles that the products aren't that alien to you.

Fishing Lures

1. _____

2. _____

3. _____

4. _____

Pinot Noir

1. _____

2. _____

3. _____

4. _____

Bridal Magazines

1. _____

2. _____

3. _____

4. _____

Organic Vegetables

1. _____

2. _____

3. _____

4. _____

Pregnancy Pants

1. _____

2. _____

3. _____

4. _____

How would you grade yourself with the new items? Are you improving? Did your friend have any moments of confusion? Was he impressed by your clear and concise directions? Does it feel natural to not merely locate various items, but convey the easiest way to find them? Do you want to grab your second friend and repeat locating fishing lures and wine? If so, you're getting the hang of it.

Now let's go for a few odd products that might come up only once in your entire career as a People Greeter. Are you ready for this expert challenge?

Fake Flowers

1. _____

2. _____

3. _____

4. _____

Plastic Gas Can

1. _____

2. _____

3. _____

4. _____

Red Lobster Gift Cards

1. _____

2. _____

3. _____

4. _____

Goldfish (baked)

1. _____

2. _____

3. _____

4. _____

Goldfish (live)

1. _____

2. _____

3. _____

4. _____

Refrigerator Magnets

1. _____

2. _____

3. _____

4. _____

Ironing Board

1. _____

2. _____

3. _____

4. _____

How did your directions turn out when you tested them with a friend? Did you get him to ironing board section? Are you feeling excited at your expertise? Don't get too cocky because that was just a practice for the real test. The real job doesn't allow you to write down the directions for every customer with a question. You must tell them. They must remember. This is tricky because people vary in their ability to understand things they're told.

The most important thing to remember when telling the directions is to not lose contact with a customer's eyes. Do not turn your back on the person and talk. It's a big store and your voice will be absorbed by a display of tube socks. Stand facing the person and feel free to point and gesture behind you. You need to make sure that they are following each of the four directions. If you sense they are slightly hazy with your concise wording; politely repeat them as if it were part of your personality. Most people won't normally admit if they didn't catch your direction. They're embarrassed that they can't grasp it. You can't let them walk away with only a partial clue. They might be too timid to admit that they zoned out on you, but they will complain to the manager that you go them lost. They'll be upset that you wasted their time even if it's their fault they ended up on the wrong side of the store.

Your only real defense to such an accusation of incompetence is to quickly to relay to your supervisor the direct and concise directions you gave out. Supervisors understand that the customer can be clueless when given directions.

You will have customers that will ask several times for you to repeat the directions. They remain unable to orient themselves in the vastness of the store. Even simple directions aren't a help. Maybe what they need is just a few steps away. The temptation is to grab their hand and lead them up the mountain of merchandise like a sherpa in blue and khaki. But your job is not to be a tour guide. You should never leave your post except for scheduled breaks or permission from a supervisor. If you sense the customer has severe issues with understanding directions or short term memory, carefully point them towards the customer service desk so that a fellow associate can be their tour guide. Don't feel bad that you couldn't do your job. You did your job. The customer might always be right, but that isn't a good thing when they need to turn left.

You must repeat the expert item questions with a different friend, but only tell them the directions. Do not let them write down the directions. Can they can navigate the store based off their memory of what you said? You're doing well if they fill up their cart based off your voice.

What should you do if a customer asks for a certain brand and you have a major suspicion that it's not stocked on the shelf? Never tell them that they might want to visit a competitor. Instead give them directions to where similar products are displayed. Odds are that once they get back to the section and notice an absence of their desired brand, they'll settle for a different brand of similar quality. Does it make you feel guilty to lie to them? You might want to give the following disclaimer in such a situation: "We add new brands so often that there's a chance that we carry it." Does that make you feel better?

What would directions be if a customer asked for the latest issue of Playboy magazine?

1. _____

2. _____

3. _____

4. _____

That's a trick question. Walmart doesn't carry any magazines that feature nudity. There are plenty of other informative magazines on the checkout aisles.

Even after you've landed the job as People Greeter, you should never stop pushing a cart around all the aisles. You need to keep up with everything that's offered. You need to always be familiar with the special displays on the endcaps and positioned in the aisles. These conveniently located presentations can make your directions even more simple. The last thing you want to do is give a customer directions where they walk past a display of the tomato soap they crave.

While it seems like a humongous undertaking, this constant tracking of products keeps your mind active. This is a prime benefit of the job that your brain won't turn completely to mush. As you get older, anything that keeps you thinking is a benefit.

The big thing to remember when giving directions is to not turn into the product's infomercial host. Do not volunteer sales prices or testimonials. Don't recommend a cheaper brand. You're there to assist and not be a salesperson. Your salary doesn't hinge on commission so don't worry about what they buy. Your job is to just get them to the shelf so they can fill up their shopping cart. The last thing you need to do is mention a sale price that's expired. You don't need to have a customer complaining to a supervisor that they want the price you promised.

In the near future there will be smart phone applications involving GPS that will allow a customer to not only build a shopping list, but locate every item. Your task of giving directions won't matter to these people. This doesn't mean you can abandon the responsibility of keeping up with product locations. Odds are increasingly high that your loyal customers will be the people who don't care for newfangled gadgets. The more unstable will swear that such a program is merely a way for the government to track their movements. They'll always demand their directions from a human being. While that sounds like a Luddite response, their attitude shall keep you employed as a People Greeter.

POP QUIZ

1) A People Greeter Gives Directions to:

    A. The bathroom

    B. The pharmacy

    C. The beer cooler

    D. Anything a customer wants to buy.

2) How many directions should you give a customer?

    A. 2

    B. 7

    C. 4

    D. Why must I limit my knowledge?

3) If a customer doesn't understand your directions

    A. They're stupid.

    B. They're hopeless.

    C. They need to go back to elementary school.

    D. They are sent to customer service for further help.

4) If a customer wants a brand not stocked by Walmart, you must:

    A. Send them home empty handed.

    B. Suggest a suitable substitute.

    C. Tell them they're not shopping at Target.

    D. Direct them to where similar items are stocked and don't mention your store doesn't carry that brand.

5) The two important Spanish words to know are:

    A. el Baño and la farmacía.

    B. Cheech and Chong

    C. Chalupa and Taco

    D. Alubia and Arroz

6) If a customer wants Pepsi, but Coke is on sale, you should:

    A. Let them know Coke is cheaper.

    B. Swear Pepsi isn't as cool as Coke.

    C. Warn them of the evils of too much sugar in their diet.

    D. Direct them to the nearest Pepsi display.

7) Where are the Maraschino Cherries?

1. _____

2. _____

3. _____

4. _____

8) Where is Puppy Chow?

1. _____

2. _____

3. _____

4. _____

9) Where is the Dehydrated Water?

1. _____

2. _____

3. _____

4. _____

10) Where are the shoelaces?

1. _____

2. _____

3. _____

4. _____

ANSWER KEY

1) **D.** - You can't be selective in your knowledge about the products stocked by Walmart.

2) **C.** - Don't confuse people with more than four directions. They shouldn't have to make more turns inside the store than it took them to drive to your store.

3) **D.** - You can't help people who have no sense of direction and a limited short term memory. They must be sent to customer service to get further assistance.

4) **D.** - Is there really that much of difference between brands? Customers will easily forget their brand loyalty when they see a great low price on a label.

5) **A.** - The bathroom and pharmacy are the only things you need to understand in Spanish since those are places people need to urgently visit.

6) **D.** - Your job is not to promote products, but to relax customers so they're in a buying mood. Give them directions and let the amazing prices do their work.

7) Check this answer on your next visit to Walmart.

8) This is with the dog food.

9) Did you not go camping as a child? The dehydrated water is stocked right next to the snipe hunting kits and left handed smoke shifters.

10) Shoelaces are in the shoe section and sometimes stocked in the checkout lanes.

SECRET FIVE: DON'T GET ATTACHED

What's the key to being a great department store Santa Claus? Make every kid think they've spent hours with Saint Nick when it's just barely enough time to read their Christmas list and smile for the photo. The line must flow without the kids thinking they're being zipped down a conveyor belt for a few seconds next to the red coat. They want to feel that their time with Santa was meaningful and special and not part of a process. What's Santa's secret? The man with the beard creates a sense of intimate brevity. How is it possible? A simple four step procedure turns a few seconds into a satisfying encounter.

1. Santa uses a warm greeting to connect with the child.

2. Santa asks the child what they want and actively listens to the answer.

3. Santa promises their wishes will be addressed on the morning of December 25 as long as they're good boys and girls.

4. Santa reminds the child that they'll see each other next year as the elf helps the child return their adult guardian.

Think back to your last visit to Santa as either a kid or a parent. Doesn't that sum up the encounter?

Let's make Santa's four step approach even more concise so it can be easily memorized:

1. Engage.

2. Exchange.

3. Assure.

4. Detach.

Four simple steps make every child in line at the Mall's North Pole embassy feel like they've had the most magical time of their life with Santa. Ask how long they talked with Santa and the children will overestimate scant minutes by hours. Why? They bonded. Santa really listened to them and promised that the gifts are on the way. Before they part ways, Santa let him know that he's always around even if the child can't see him so this isn't really a goodbye. Hopefully letting you in on this secret has not destroyed your special childhood memories of meeting Santa. Don't stress out and question what was really true in your youth. Santa's real, but he had a system to get his work done. If every child talked to him for hours, Christmas would come once a decade.

A Walmart People Greeter can be viewed as "Santa Claus in navy blue and khaki." Instead of children, the Greeter has adults eagerly asking for a special item on their list that they really, really need. Unlike Santa, a Greeter won't be coming down their chimney with the item. They have to get it themselves. We have already covered how to warmly greet, ask what a customer wants and address their needs. You have mastered Steps One, Two and Three. The last step is a major secret in being a successful greeter. You can't focus on incoming customers with people permanently attached to you.

There's a paradox to the job that might confuse an applicant. A Greeter is paid to be social, but isn't supposed to socialize. They need to talk to the customers, but avoid engaging in a real conversation. What's the difference between talking and conversing? Sometimes it's hard to say. But a quick rule is that if you feel like you're having a conversation with a customer; you're having a conversation with a customer. You're having a conversation if you catch yourself saying, "Let me tell you about the time I...." If your answer must include personal details, you're having a conversation. A Greeter should never imagine he is hosting a talkshow being broadcast around the globe thanks to the security cameras. Perhaps someday a cable network will create a reality show about a Greeter, but you don't need the loss prevention team to cut your audition tape. You are under no obligation to turn every customer into your new best friend. All they need to know is that a friendly person works there and can help them. Do not delude them into thinking they can drop by anytime and shoot the breeze while you're working up front.

You should never be responsible for a bottleneck at the entrance of the store. The only reason for a line in front of you is a freakish amount of customers returning items at once. The post-Christmas period is notorious for returns, but stores implement special a traffic flow pattern to handle it. You must never delay customers who are eager to purchase as soon as they get directions. The Greeter must make sure that customers don't linger around the entrance. You can't afford to have a never-ending dialogue with a pal or associate while another customer with a simple question is forced to wait. Even worse is having two or more customers impatiently waiting while a long winded customer keeps talking and avoids shopping. This is what brings you to the attention of a supervisor or two.

How do you get a customer to detach when you've answered their questions? You must use a painless method that won't let you been seen as rude or heartless. They need to happily proceed into the store to enjoy the wide world of shopping. Your method must be done at a level quieter than the tearing noise from separating Velcro. Don't reflect completely on what Santa does to get stubborn kids detached. Santa has it easy. If a child refuses to get off Santa's lap, trained elves surgically remove the clinger from your lap and politely guide the child back to his parents. You have no elf bouncers to drag away customers who can't take a hint. You have to rely on yourself. You have to avoid any consumer drama. Customers are accustomed to shouting and threats at the customer service desk. That's a major reason why they'll approach the people greeter with a simple question instead of being stuck behind a dysfunctional talkshow guest audition.

All walks of life pass through the electronic eye opening doors. Your job is keep them walking. Most of the time, customers getting attached to you isn't an issue. Ninety five percent of the people entering Walmart will refuse to acknowledge your existence or barely give you a passing hello as they head straight to the merchandise. A little over four percent will ask for directions to a product and speed away with a quick thanks. Like Ivory Soap, 99 44/100% of your customer interactions will be extremely brief encounters. However it's the 0.56% that will become bothersome. They will attempt to latch onto you like a leech on a vein. You can't afford to have them drain you while the shift clock is ticking.

Which of these people can cause a conflict that might lead to losing your prestigious People Greeter position? How can you identify them and defuse them before they explode like a bomb if they sense you're detaching them? You must be able to identify them fast and thus avoid a hazardous situation. Here's a breakdown of the types of people who have no problem clogging up the line and detachment moves to keep them from sticking to you.

FRIENDS AND FAMILY

Those close to you might not seem like a problem, but they're the first batch of people eager to jam up the entrance while occupying your attention. They're used to your old job. They called you during the work day and got right through to your private line. You would close your office door and fake like it was an important business client. None of your co-workers could tell and none of them cared since they were handling their own personal calls on the company phone. Friends dropped by your old office to enjoy your endless lunch hour. They remember how you took pleasure in figuring out ways to goof off on the clock with the company's expense account. As long as it seemed like business, nobody questioned your actions. Sadly enough, those days are over. A People Greeter can't shut the doors for personal time with friends and family. Your new "office" is completely open with all eyes on you. There's no looking busy while slacking off on your duties. You will be noticed.

Your friends and family have to realize that you won't be immediately answering your phone calls during your shift. You can't stand at the station talking or texting on a cellphone while ignoring incoming customers. Your cellphone is off. Don't even be tempted to merely put it on vibrate. You don't need to know if someone is calling. Don't allow yourself to sneak a peek when you think no one is watching you. Thanks to the security camera, you're always being watched. You don't need a supervisor to go to the tape to show your cellphone issue is habitual and the reason for you being dismissed. You must wait until your mandated breaks or the end of your shift before powering up the cellphone and returning messages.

What if your family member or friend needs to contact you with important news that needs an immediate response? If it's a real emergency, they should call the store and have you paged. What constitutes a real emergency? Solid reasons for them to call you during your shift include your spouse being taken away in an ambulance, a liver donor has been located or your important medication was left on the kitchen table. Where you left the cable remote is not an emergency. Do make sure that you check the messages on your cellphone before leaving work since there might be a call wanting you to pick up food for dinner. After a long shift, you don't need to drive back to Walmart for last minute groceries.

Family and Friends dropping by your Greeter station can be tough. Instinctually you'll want to drop everything and talk to them like the good old days. You'll get the urge to give them the tour of your new "office." But you can't leave your post or ignore incoming customers that aren't familiar faces. If they invite you out to lunch, you'll be two steps toward the door before the harsh reality slams you in the stomach. You no longer control your lunch break. You can't slip out the front door and have your secretary take messages. You can always tell your family and friends when your lunch break is scheduled in case they want to stick around. But they need to know that you're due back at your post at a fixed time. Don't get too depressed at this. You'll have plenty of time for long lunches when you get to completely retire.

How do you get family and friends to understand that you can't just stand around and shoot the breeze? Since they are family and friends, you have to be truthful and blunt with them. Explain to them that you must focus on your People Greeter duties. They should be able to understand your request. If a family member can't handle an obvious request, warn them that you'll never let them near your employee discount. That threat ought to get them scurrying into the aisles.

DUCKS

This isn't about waterfowl sneaking through the front doors, although a few stores have an issue with non-migrating Canadian geese squatting in their parking lots. Ducks are people you barely know and really wish you didn't know. You've met them through a friend of a friend at a ballgame or public event. Somehow they follow the rule that a friend of a friend is also their friend. Only, you find these people annoying, tedious and frustrating. You can't completely freeze them out since they'll complain to your mutual friend and cause a scene. Their dramatic nature really annoys you. The best way to avoid confrontations is to duck behind something. You'll duck in the bathroom, duck under a table for a "lost" contact lens and duck into the trunk of your car. You know that the minute they spot you, the torture of their mundanity will be inflicted on your soul.

If you had the position of a normal associate job on the floor and spotted the Duck, you'd come up with an excuse to flee into the storage freezer and count the case of dehydrated ice cubes. Abandoning the People Greeter station to avoid being spotted by the Duck isn't an option. Even if you signal that you need an emergency toilet break, you'll have to wait for your replacement long enough for the Duck to spot you. You're a sitting duck for the Duck. There's an outside chance that they might not recognize you in the navy blue and khaki dress code. This is a good time to apply a robotic welcome so that they don't come close to sensing that you know each other. If you're lucky, you'll be ignored as someone who looks like someone they know.

This tactic won't work if your mutual friend is a big mouth that announces to the Duck that you're now a People Greeter. You'll have to resort to Plan B. What Plan B can possibly work on someone who knows you have no escape from their conversation? Ask them if they want to have a meal, coffee or beers after your shift. It might sound drastic, but odds are high that they're going to have to bail on your offer. They don't want to be that much of a friend. After their decline, you make a simple closing statement that includes seeing them at your mutual friend's upcoming gathering. Immediately lose eye contact with them and greet an incoming customer. The duck will take the clue and fly into the store.

THE CHURCH LADY

A few of your casual contacts will view you as a great resource for gathering information to stand in moral judgment of others. The Church Lady can also be a man who needs to get dirt on an acquaintance. They'll hit you up for stories about mutual friends that might have been recently shopping in the store. They'll act all nice and innocent when asking about the third party. "Do they shop here a lot?" They'll slowly want to know if this person shops with other people who may or may not be their spouse. They view you as a way to confirm rumors of an extramarital affair. They'll pump you for the shopping habits of others. Do you remember if a mutual friend finally bought a widescreen TV, a riding lawnmower or organic groceries? While you might know the answers, you can't tell them a thing. You're a People Greeter and not a People Blabbermouth. Part of your job is discretion. You want to spoil a Christmas surprise by telling the wrong person what you saw in an outgoing shopping buggy? The only reason you should admit to seeing someone shopping is if they're are the subject of an Amber or Silver Alert.

Avoid telling the Church Lady that you can't share details of customers and their buggies. This denial of information will sound more like a tease and entice The Church Lady to be more persistent. Never elevate the drama. How do you get out of the third degree questioning? Claim the day is a blur and you can't even remember if it's Tuesday or Wednesday. Use the "senior moment" excuse to your advantage when it comes to why you don't remember people and their purchases. They'll stop talking to you once they recognize you won't be their undercover informant. The only bad part of this tactic is the Church Lady might spread a rumor that you're losing your memory. This is a better fate than having a furious ex-friend attack you in the parking lot for disclosing their shopping companion.

DRESS REHEARSAL CAST

People can be intimidated by the Customer Service Desk when asking for their money back. They're anxious with a fear of being told that they screwed up and are stuck with the unwanted product. In order to avoid rejection, they practice their routine until they are smooth enough to avoid any resistance at the Customer Service Desk. They need to test their performance on an out-of-town audience like a Broadway play. The People Greeter has mistakenly been accepted as the best place to work out the kinks. Most will try out their excuse while you log and tag the return item. There's nothing wrong with them giving their spiel unless they keep going after you're done.

Out-of-Town performances have a knack for running too long. Many times, the customer will repeat themselves to tighten up their tale of why the shoes don't match their favorite outfit. It's like they want to win a Tony and not merely get $19.95 charged back to their credit card.

Their rehearsal invites you to critique their performance and presentation like a focus group member that gives notes to a producer before opening night. It's nice that they want you to care, but don't make suggestions for what can get trimmed or lines that ring hollow. You must be an impartial observer. Allow yourself to be more focused on logging the return and oblivious to their excuse. It's OK to zone them out like a reverse mortgage commercial or a boring relative.

The customer craves for you to say, "You'll be getting your money back without any problems." But don't give them any assurances about their chances for success. You're not there to predict outcomes. The last thing you need to hear shouted from the Customer Service Desk is, "But the People Greeter swore you'd give me a cash refund!" That outburst will get you in trouble with your supervisor. Don't feel guilty only giving answers that push the burden on the Customer Service associates. You have enough duties without doing their job.

What should you do if the customer's rehearsed explanation keeps unwinding after their item has been logged? You are under no obligation to hear the entire story. Feel free to politely cut them off when your task is done. Interrupt them by saying, "Now Customer Service can assist you." Make sure you point directly at the nearby Customer Service Desk so they get the overwhelming hint that their time with you is over. The Dress Rehearsal Cast Member is ready to take their routine to the big stage.

THE CHEAP PATIENT

During cold and flu season, the walking sick shall lumber through the doors in search of quick over-the-counter fixes at the pharmacy or an examination at Urgent Care (not featured at all locations). Most of them understand their contagious condition and will maintain a safe distance if they need directions. An undesirable few will get close to you. They don't merely want to inquire about the pharmacy location. Their intention is to seek a diagnosis from you.

Why have they mistaken you for a physician? A simple answer is that you're old. The sick customer figures that the elderly have either had what they've had or once had a friend that survived the same symptoms. Why waste money on a doctor giving a mouthful of medical mumbo jumbo and a scribbled prescription note for an overpriced bottle of pills? They can't be bothered with an Urgent Care physician since there's a wait, paperwork and co-pay. An ill customer swears the People Greeter can give them real advice with a cheaper solution in record time. You've replaced Dr. Mom in their mind.

The first rule is to not let these people get within arm's reach of you. Feel free to take a step back if they invade your personal space. Maintain eye contact while retreating so they don't think you're running away. You must remain polite and calm no matter how much they appear like a germy monster on a mission to infect you. You might not know what they have, but you know you're too damn old to catch whatever it is. You don't need to burn your sick days on second hand germs.

The second rule is to avoid any level of examination of the customer. Under no circumstances can you look at a body part if they ask, "Does this look infected?" You can't afford to spend the rest of your shift remembering their running sores. They may insist on describing their aches, pains and mucus levels, but you must avoid any pretense of an answer. Don't give them any medical advice even if you were formerly a doctor, nurse, EMT, technical advisor to General Hospital or army medic. Why? Because you don't need to deal with a malpractice lawsuit or be arrested for practicing medicine without a license. You barely have enough time for lunch. In the case that your store has an Urgent Care, you can't be accused as stealing their business. That doesn't mean you must be completely oblivious to their condition like a heartless robot. Feel free to have 911 alerted if the customer is profusely bleeding, holding a limb, turning a deep shade of blue or projectile vomiting. Anything that doesn't require immediate attention from the rescue squad; your answer should always be, "You need to talk to the pharmacist" or "Our urgent care can help you." Stick to those lines. Repeat them to any persistent customer who refuses to admit that People Greeters aren't emergency room doctors.

Under all circumstances, feel free to apply hand sanitizer to any parts of your body that might have been contaminated by the unwell. Remember to wait until they've dragged their sickly carcass to the pharmacy or urgent care. You don't want them to feel insulted.

THE PACKAGE TOUR

By this point, you know exactly how direct a customer to any item in the store. Most shoppers need your four simple directions and away they scamper. However there will be a few customers that will arrive with a shopping list. They will beg you to give them directions to everything on that list. You don't have time to be a tour guide or personal shopper. Like an express lane, you can only help on three items or less.

There's two ways to treat the person with the long list. The first is to direct them to the nearest requested item. Insist that an associate in that area can help them locate the next item. Once they check off one item on their list, they'll receive the confidence to find everything else on their own. They won't bother any other associates. If they do get lost in the store there are plenty of associates on the floor eager to help. If you sense the customer truly needs a guide to make it around the store then you must resort to the second way. Direct them to Customer Service Desk. They can assign an associate to make sure the customer has a comfortable shopping experience. You don't want them to leave the store without everything on the list appearing on their receipt.

THE TALK RADIO FANATIC

Most customers drive a few miles to the store. While many people enjoy singing along with music on the radio, others shout at political talk shows. Why do they have to get angry and upset by a stranger's voice? Perhaps their caffeine intake hasn't gotten their blood pressure soaring high enough for them to shop? They're frustrated by not being able to call into the radio station to voice their correct point of view over the airwaves. They're juiced up about a topic and ready to vent. Your saying, "Welcome to Walmart" will be misconstrued as "You're on the air, caller!"

If a customer replies, "Did you just hear..." brace yourself for a synopsis of what they just heard on the radio. Maybe they can't reach millions of listeners, but they're eager to take control of your ears. Feel free to cut them off if the news isn't about an impending weather event, traffic jam or famous person's death. You don't need a second hand accounting of a talk radio host or politician's spiel. The customer isn't going to tell you and run. They'll want you to validate their opinion by asking you your feeling of the topic. Under no circumstances do you express a political belief to a customer. You might fully agree with the position they expound, but you can't show it. There's an outside chance they're just baiting you so they can pull off the rebuttal they concocted in the car. They're going to get louder and louder as they talk so that everyone in the store can hear their genius reply to you. While you don't work in a library, you never want management to warn you about unnecessary noise.

What's the best way to cut off the talk radio caller? It's time to play the old person card, again. Explain to them that you must avoid the news because you suffer from high blood pressure. If you get too upset by current events, you'll die. That should give them a quick message that you don't care what they heard on the radio.

What about the sports talk radio fanatic wanting to talk to you? You still need to avoid the conversation. There's a chance you'll pick the wrong team and they're going to let you know it very loudly. You don't want incoming customers to think they've entered a sports bar during happy hour. If they persist, once more play the old person card to stop the conversation. Claim that you no longer follow sports since your favorite players are dead.

There is a good conversation that can be based on what a customer heard on the radio. This happens when the customer asks where to find the music department so they can buy the song they heard on the drive to the store.

THE NOSTALGIC

A customer might ask you where to find a Powerhouse candy bar. It sounds like a simple request, but it's a trick question. You can only find it after you locate the store's time machine. They stopped making Powerhouse in the late '80s. If you know this fact, the customer will immediately start remembering other products that are gone from the shelves behind you. This customer loves to wax nostalgic and they want you to be riding shotgun during their trip down memory lane. It's so warm and inviting to fall into their conversational trap about how much cooler food, drink, toys and music was when both of you were younger. You'll get engrossed in a game of "Do you remember?"

What could be wrong with spending a short time reminiscing on the clock? The chat with nostalgic customer will give you a warm tingle, but it won't stay that way. You'll think back to those carefree times when you bought Powerhouse candy bars in high school. Then you'll wonder what wrong steps you took that put you in the shoes of a People Greeter. You'll reflect on your youthful ambitions and potential. You'll get frustrated when you catch your mature reflection in a nearby mirror. The thought of a single Powerhouse candy bar will sap your strength as it sits in your stomach. You can't allow the nostalgic customer to drag you down with regrets. Send them to the department where similar items are stocked and avoid the historical chit-chat.

THE SIDEKICK

Ever notice a familiar faces roaming the store during the day always eager to help confused customers. They'll straighten up displays that have been ravaged by kids. They enjoy spending time at the entrance asking how things are going. They don't mind offering up answers to a customer needing directions when you're busy logging a return. They sound like the perfect nominee for employee of the month. Why would these people be a problem? Because they aren't real employees.

These helpful customers fancy themselves as an unofficial Walmart Greeters. Why won't they apply for the job? Maybe they have an issue with working under a manager? Perhaps they prefer to show up and leave on their own schedule? They might imagine themselves as the elves that help the shoemaker. Maybe they've been rejected at a different store for having a black mark on their work record, but they can't stifle their desire to work at Walmart? It's hard to tell. The fact that they have volunteered to be your sidekick is an issue.

They will hang around your station craving inside information about the store and employees. The questions might be innocent like unannounced store hours for the upcoming holiday season or the birthdays of your fellow People Greeters. Under no circumstances should you share such information with an outsider. Do not feed the sidekick's delusion that they're an employee.

While it seems tempting, never let a sidekick escort a customer to find a product. Do nothing that will make them feel like they're really your sidekick. Since they are a customer, having them hang around your station for prolonged periods of time doesn't look good. A People Greeter works alone and if they need help, it's someone on the payroll.

The best way to scare a sidekick off is have the supervisor bring over a job application. Tell the sidekick that you'll give them a recommendation. This makes them know that you're not upset at them. You merely want them to be able to fully enjoy their time hanging out at Walmart. Handing them the job application will send the simple message that a sidekick better join up or ship out. Odds are high they'll move onto the nearest Walmart to continue their sidekick ways, but at least it's not your Walmart.

GROUPIES

Hard to believe, but you might become the object of lust from strangers. As you stand at your station you might notice a customer becoming more familiar with you. They are friendlier in their response after you welcome them to Walmart. You might swear they are flirting with you during the brief conversation. They just might be flirting.

A simple glance on the internet reveals a multitude of people who have a fetish for the military, police and firefighters. If their libidos are excited by uniforms, there must be a few folks excited by employees sticking to a dress code. A navy blue shirt and khaki pants might be oysters and champagne to the right person. Can you handle being an object of lust?

This might be a new experience if you never had strangers drop by the office and unleash their eyes on you. You'll feel like a rock star when groupies sneak backstage. They're yours for the asking. Don't ever hook up with a groupie no matter how enticing they are. Consider it a compliment that they're flirting with you and leave it at that.

What could possibly go wrong? If they are turned on by hooking up with a Walmart People Greeter, they're not going to like it when you don't wear the Navy Blue and Khaki. They might act like you're a stranger if you wear a red shirt and blue jeans on a date. You really want to dress like a Greeter when you're not on the clock? You want someone attracted to you and not your adherence to a dress code.

Things can get worse if your affair with the Groupie goes bad. They know where you work. The last thing you need is for them to show up and cause a scene at the entrance. How can you explain to management why someone just went nuts at your station? They're not going to like knowing you're abusing your high profile position by hooking up with customers. Always remember that nothing good can come from sleeping with Groupies.

What can you do to avoid being the target of Groupies? Always wear your wedding ring. Buy a cheap wedding ring if you are currently single. If a suspected Groupie asks what you're doing on your day off; the answer should be either a friend's funeral or a grandchild's birthday. They'll get the message that you're not interested in a relationship after clocking out for the day. They'll just move onto the People Greeter assigned to the next shift. They're not in it for your heart, but being close to the khaki and navy blue.

THE DISTRACTOR

Most shoplifters act alone. They snag an item in a moment of desperation or overwhelmed by their kleptomania. These lone wolves with sticky fingers are only your problem if they set off the security gate. You ask for their receipt. If you find a wrong item in their bag, they get to explain it all to loss prevention. What you really have to worry about is when it becomes a team sport. Professional shoplifters work in units with a shopping list of what's perfect for a five finger discount. Members are given duties to insure victory over store security like a sports team. The distractor's sole job it to occupy your attention while the gang escapes.

Shoplifters are under the mistaken belief that you're the last hurdle in their sprint to escape with their loot. If they can sneak it past you, they're home free. You already know that is not the case. You're too old to chase, grab and tackle these kids. Your days of playing cornerback on the football field are long gone. You still need to watch out for the distractor since they're going to bring the game to you.

The more benign Distractor will merely lurk around the entrance until they see their crew approach. They will toss an active security tag into the cart of an outgoing customer to have them set off the alarm on the gate. While you're asking the innocent customer for their receipt, the shoplifting team sneaks out. If the crew is stealing items that aren't security tagged, the distractor might merely start talking to you and ever so slowly turn so your eyes will follow them and miss his pals streaking out the front door. After they exit, the Distractor shops like a normal customer.

Sometimes a Distractor will get more dramatic by using the classic seizure move. They'll flop on the floor and fake a series of spasms. You'll want to assist along with other customers who think they know First Aid. In the confusion, the shoplifters make a quick break. If someone has a seizure in front of you, immediately alert your supervisor that you have a medical emergency. Do not treat the seizure victim as a Distractor and accuse them of faking it. They might really be suffering from a seizure. The last thing you need to be is targeted in the local media as the mean People Greeter who refused to help a seizure victim.

The most frightening thing a Distractor might do is to punch you in the face. The Distractor thinks that taking you out with a sucker punch is the best distraction. They know people will be more concerned with your broken jaw and bleeding mouth than his buddies bolting out the exit with cases of beer. This is a reason why you should always keep an arm's length between you and a customer. Always have enough space behind you to step back in case they take a swing.

You can't stop a Distractor since they aren't shoplifting. But you can spook them acting like you know them. The last thing they need to fear is that you might know where they live and can pass that information to the cops. That's when they go from Distractor to disability on their team. They'll target another store.

MENTAL ISSUES

There are customers with various psychological issues that will talk to you. This might vary from people who want you to reveal the conspiracies of Walmart to those with difficulty communicating. Be patient with these customers. Supervisors should cut you a bit of slack if they linger around your station longer than the average customer. They don't want complaints that the store hates people with mental issues.

YOU

You can easily be the reason the entrance line bottlenecks. Ever notice how much quicker the workday goes when you're having a good talk with someone? It's tempting to strike up a conversation with a customer when you sense it's going to be a slow time during your shift. You don't want to stand there alone. You're open to engaging the Nostalgic. But you can't start talking to make the clock hands move faster. You're not hired to be the People Gabber. The last thing you need is for your supervisor to view you as the Greeter who just won't shut up. Keep non-essential conversations with the customers to a minimum.

You can't allow yourself to get attached to the customers. You don't need to share anything about yourself with them. Unlike a job in sales where you expose biographical details to create a bond with your client, a People Greeter can remain mysterious. All a customer needs to know about you is that you can help them if they need to find or return an item. Don't be your most annoying customer.

Whenever you're in doubt, just ask yourself how Santa would deal with this customer so the line can keep moving.

POP QUIZ

1) What holiday icon should you pattern yourself after?

    A. The Easter Bunny

    B. Santa

    C. Baby New Year

    D. The Great Pumpkin

2) What type of customers are you eager to ignore?

    A. Ducks

    B. Geese

    C. Bears

    D. Sharks

3) When old friends visit, you should:

    A. Take an extended lunch break.

    B. Shoot the breeze.

    C. Send them to get you a drink.

    D. Let them know when your shift ends.

4) The reason to tell a Church Lady about mutual friend's visit:

    A. You think they're having an affair.

    B. You want to spoil their big Christmas surprise.

    C. You fear they've been drinking.

    D. There's a missing person's report filed on them.

5) What are the four steps to treating a customer?

    _____

    _____

    _____

    _____

6) What do you do with a customer who wants you to diagnosis their sickness?

    A. Feel their forehead.

    B. Use a smart phone to check their symptoms.

    C. Relate it to a sickness you've had in the past.

    D. Send them to the Pharmacy without any medical advice.

7) How many items will you direct a customer to find?

    A. One.

    B. Two.

    C. Three.

    D. Infinity.

s8) If a customer asks you about politics, your response will be:

    A. Honest.

    B. Loud.

    C. Harsh.

    D. No comment.

9) The problem with talking to a Nostalgic customer is:

    A. You'll want to go shopping for antiques.

    B. You'll get hungry for Power House candy bars.

    C. You'll wonder why you've become People Greeter.

    D. He'll become your new best friend.

10) Groupies are:

    A. Dangerous.

    B. Tempting.

    C. A perk of the job.

    D. Really in love with you.

11) Distractors will:

    A. Smile at you.

    B. Bring you gifts.

    C. Confess quickly to their criminal enterprise.

    D. Punch you in the face.

12) What you have to worry most about is:

    A. The Church Lady.

    B. The Distractor.

    C. The Nostalgic.

    D. You.

ANSWER KEY

1) **B**. - Don't let anyone sit on your lap.

2) **A**. - If only you can pluck them upon arrival.

3) **D**. - You can catch up on your own time..

4) **D**. - You're not paid to gossip.

5) Engage, Exchange, Assure and Detach.

6) **D**. - You're a People Greeter and not a doctor.

7) **C**. - The position isn't personal shopper.

8) **D**. - You're not hired to be pundit.

9) **C**. - Don't get sucked in a nostalgia whirlpool.

10) **A**. -Nothing good can come from groupie attention.

11) **D**. - Don't let them get close to your face.

12) **D**. - You can't let yourself be the gabber.

SECRET SIX: DON'T REFLECT THE HATE

The myth presents a Walmart People Greeter as a highly beloved person in America. The kind, mature employee with a helpful attitude for every customer and a smile for all the kids seems plucked from Disneyland's Main Street U.S.A. There's a warm nostalgic element to the position. How can someone not like such a person? The People Greeter should receive the same level of respect as astronauts and grandparents at a family reunion picnic. Sadly this is not perception held by numerous Walmart customers and co-workers.

Here's a charming little story that became a well-forwarded email:

```
Jennifer a manager at Walmart had the task
of hiring someone to fill a job opening.
After sorting through a stack of 20 resumes
she found four people who were equally
qualified. Jennifer decided to call the four
in and ask them only one question. Their
answer would determine which of them would
get the job.

The day came and as the four sat around the
conference room table, Jennifer asked, "What
is the fastest thing you know of?"
```

The first man replied, "A thought. It just pops into your head. There's no warning."

"That's very good!" replied Jennifer. "And, now you sir?," she asked the second man.

"Hmmm.....let me see. A blink! It comes and goes and you don't know that it ever happened. A blink is the fastest thing I know of."

"Excellent!" said Jennifer. "The blink of an eye, that's a very popular cliché for speed." She then turned to the third man, who was contemplating his reply.

"Well, out at my dad's ranch, you step out of the house and on the wall there's a light switch. When you flip that switch, way out across the pasture the light on the barn comes on in less than an instant. Yip, turning on a light is the fastest thing I can think of."

Jennifer was very impressed with the third answer and thought she had found her man. "It's hard to beat the speed of light," she said.

Turning to Bubba, the fourth and final man, Jennifer posed the same question.

Old Bubba replied, "After hearing the previous three answers, it's obvious to me that the fastest thing known is diarrhea."

'What!?' said Jennifer, stunned by the response.

"Oh sure," said Bubba. "You see, the other day I wasn't feeling so good, and I ran for

```
the bathroom, but before I could think,
blink or turn on the light, I had already
pooped my pants."

Bubba is now the new greeter at a Walmart in
Dewpoint, NC.! You probably will think of
this every time you enter a Walmart from now
on.
```

What did you think of that joke? Did you laugh? It might be funny at this moment because you're not a Walmart People Greeter. You may begin to feel a sense of regret in laughing when you take your first shift at the Greeter station. You've invested a serious amount of time into finding what skills are necessary to be a great greeter. Why would you want to dedicate so much time for a position that bowel control impaired Bubba landed? You know there's more to being the right person for the position than confessing that you've pooped your pants.

How would you react if someone told you that joke after you'd been hired as a greeter?

    A) Roll your eyes.

    B) Politely laugh.

    C) Hearty laugh.

    D) Punch them in the face.

The only wrong answer is D. A person's natural instinct is to defend your honor when insulted. You can deliver a passionate explanation of the mental and physical demands of the position. You could tell the comedian to shut up since his joke wasn't funny. Or you might slap some sense into his numbskull for disrespecting your workplace. This is an extremely wrong response. A People Greeter isn't a People Beater. You need to be calm and good natured to hold the job. Nothing can get you upset in public.

You can't reflect the hate given to you by customers, co-workers or the world in general. You need to be maintain a cheerful attitude under all circumstances. You're hired to be happy. When you stand at the entrance of the store, you must be the happiest person on the Earth. Every day is the greatest day of your life. You want incoming customers to bask in the sunshine beaming out of your face. Is this a natural emotion you can express? If not, can you figure out how to fake it for the entire length of your shift? Can you hold that smile when the customers cause you grief? Can you maintain a glow when co-workers trash talk you? There are going to be days when you will swear that your duties make you feel battered and abused like a rodeo clown or a dunking booth goon. They have the advantage that their smiles are maintained with greasepaint. You've got to do it with muscles and will power. Being happy is hard work that rarely gets credit from others. They think you're born with a peppy gene sort of like how a baseball player has a natural eye for hitting curveballs.

Disgruntled co-workers will treat you poorly because they don't think you perform real work to collect your paycheck. They've got to move boxes, hang clothes, sort fruit, unpack meat and quickly check out shopping carts. They perceive your job as hanging out and gabbing with customers. They swear you're not sweating like them with your social butterfly position. Even though you're beyond middle aged, these self-righteous coworkers swear you somehow haven't earned the right to not exert the same physical energy as them. You might have spent the last forty years busting your hump, but you're the shiftless newbie in their eyes. They're not going to treat you with respect in the break room. They'll alienate you from their cliques. They're not going to ask you to join them in their reindeer games. How can you remedy this situation?

A professional workplace counselor would suggest that you befriend these jerks. Perhaps offer to buy them lunch at the fast food franchise near the store entrance. During the meal, you can share the story of your life so they understand you've sacrificed for decades. A former ex-convict will tell you to merely pick out the biggest antagonist and jump them in the parking lot after work.

Neither of these are the solution since they don't address the real problem. The co-worker doesn't hate you. He hates what you represent at the greeter station.

For a majority of lifelong Walmart employees, the People Greeter is the final rung of the career ladder. Your position is the hospice of their employment tenure track. They dream of working their way into management so their wardrobe switches from the navy blue and khaki dress code to business suits. They have a fantasy about being called to the manager's office and getting told to report to a corporate office for their next gig. But for a vast majority of lifelong employees, they don't leave the store. They might shuffle between departments, but they really don't take on major responsibilities within the corporate structure. They're assigned tasks and expected to complete them within a fixed time. Their biggest nightmare is being called into the manager's office to be offered the People Greeter position. It's the equivalent of a doctor telling your co-worker the diagnosis is inoperable cancer. The end is near when they become the People Greeter. Do you really think that sharing a large order of fries is going to abate their spite of your role in the store?

What do you do? Nothing. It's their problem. It becomes your problem when you let their hostile attitude get under your skin. You could fight back by reminding them that eventually they'll be saying, "Welcome to Walmart." This will merely increase the animosity level. The co-worker might cause you bodily harm since now they'll have a reason to hate you on a personal level. The best thing you can do is ignore them like you've probably done over the decades to the office gadflies. Remember that at the end of their days, they'll be stuck in the People Greeter position. They'll be mocked as lazy by a future co-worker. They'll be trapped in a circle of hate. Sometimes the best form of revenge is to let nature take its course. If they get too nasty, have friends write nasty customer complaints about the crabby co-worker to the store manager.

The most hate you'll feel will come from random customers. Don't expect everyone to treat you as a beloved acquaintance. A majority of people will act like you don't really exist, which is also fine as long as they don't set off the security gate. Other customers shall return your welcome and treat you like a human being. What you have to be prepared to experience are the few customers out to ruin your day.

You need to approach your job with the same attitude of a lion tamer. Never let your guard down. A customer may appear to be friendly but, they have a shot at turning on you like a fierce lion. Why? Who knows. People get set off for a variety of unexpected reasons. You must be prepared for these snap moments. Unlike a lion tamer, you're not allowed to threaten customers with a bullwhip or revolver. You can only use a lion tamer's passive defensive strategies. Never allow yourself to be boxed in by a customer. The worst thing you can do is not have space to quickly step back or run into the store if a customer goes out of control. Reports of unprovoked attacks on Walmart People Greeters are in the news. A 100 year old female greeter was punched in the face by a violent customer in Milwaukee, Wisconsin. Why would someone punch a 100-year-old woman? Ultimately the answer doesn't matter. What matters is that you can't put yourself in a position where a crazed customer can sucker punch you. Don't ever let people get too close. Don't put your back up against a wall or display. Always be ready to take a step back when you don't trust a customer.

Most cranky customers are just going to verbally abuse you. A majority of these loudmouths are in a bad mood and don't have an internal mute button. Their pent up anger is released by you saying, "Welcome to Walmart!" It's an excuse for them to throw their misery in your face. They can't deal with anyone being happy when they're in a mood. Many of them were sent to the store against their will by a disgruntled partner. They are not happy to be shopping since they'd rather be watching the big game, napping on the sofa or getting drunk. They're itching for the argument they dare not have at home.

Your best defense is scoffing off their negativity with a polite, whatever attitude. Don't try to correct them. Don't give them a nasty look. Don't immediately call store security. You must remain passive to this rude attack. Don't completely ignore the person because they might be itching to elevate this clash into a full-fledged fight. Some may be under the influence of drugs or alcohol. They want the slightest response so they can drop gloves and go at you. Or they'll take your ignoring them as an insult. The best tactic is to give them a concerned look as if they really didn't mean to say that to you, but you're not expecting an apology. This should let the irritated customer know they've overstepped their bounds. They need to get what they came for and get going. If they do charge, you should be prepared to escape with your lion tamer sensibility. Immediately alert security and hope the upset customer quickly comes to their senses. Most will back down and flee in shame once they realize they're threatening a People Greeter.

After they've disappeared into the store, you need to put their insult out of your mind. You must to greet the next customer as if nothing out of the ordinary has happened. After working as a People Greeter for a few months, it will be part of the ordinary. You don't need to give the next customer the same level of grief that was smashed into you.

Happy Holidays

The time of year that elevates bad attitudes from customers is the Christmas shopping season. This isn't about the human surge that follows the doors being opened whenever the first major sales are announced. The consistent unjolly mood comes from customers who shop for gifts in the weeks before Halloween to the post-Christmas sales in January. During this season, you may wish to say, "Happy Holidays! Welcome to Walmart." There are customers who find it offensive. They aren't disgusted that you're bringing religion into their lives. They're under the impression that there's a conspiratorial "War on Christmas." They think you're part of the secular atheist terrorists because you refuse to say, "Merry Christmas."

Can this be true? Are you out to kill the spiritual meaning of Christmas and merely enforce the rampant consumerism element? Of course you are not out to destroy Christmas. A person might want to act as if Christmas is the only special day during this period, but there's plenty of other holidays. Even among Christians there's The Annunciation, Christmas Eve, Christmas Day and Epiphany. Jewish shoppers observe Hanukkah. Numerous religions have holidays at this time. Canadians have their Boxing Day. Pop culture fans partake in Festivus and Beethoven's birthday. Let's not forget Kwanza. We all celebrate New Year's Eve and New Year's Day. It's a time filled with happy holidays for everyone who shops at Walmart. Why limit your greeting when spreading holiday joy?

Should you ever wish a Merry Christmas to a customer? Feel free to say it if a customer wears a t-shirt or sweater featuring Santa, the word Christmas or a religious depiction of Christmas events. You can wish a Merry Christmas if the customer wishes you a Merry Christmas first. Otherwise stick to Happy Holidays.

If someone gives you grief for not giving them a Merry Christmas greeting just say, "Merry Christmas." They don't have any real Christmas spirit if they keep grousing afterward. They're just looking to cause trouble. If they have any lingering issues about your greeting, send them to Customer Service. Don't let them ruin your holiday cheer.

There will be days when news and events outside the Walmart will weigh heavily on you. Your doctor gives you a diagnosis for a new aliment that means more medication. A close friend dies the night before. Your boyhood home gets bulldozed to make space for a new Walmart. They cancel your favorite TV show. You're having a bad hair day. Once you enter the store, your bad day needs to be stashed in the employee locker. You need to cheer up before you punch the clock.

A People Greeter can't have a bad day. You're not permitted to be sad, grumpy or stressed. If a customer asks how you're doing, don't unload all the issues bothering you. You know why? Cause nobody needs your problems tossed into their shopping cart. The Express Lane is for 20 items or less. They have no desire to buy your emotional baggage after they load up on ground chuck and tube socks.

Here's a little playlet for you to use during your average workday when in doubt about how to respond:

GREETER: Welcome to Wal-Mart!

CUSTOMER: Thanks. How are you doing?

GEETER: Fine. Anything you're specifically looking for?

Notice that your side of the conversation immediately gets the topic back to the customer and what products they want to purchase on their visit. Nobody drives over to Walmart in order to give sympathy and advice to the People Greeter at 3 a.m. They're not practicing for their analyst or therapist license with you as their test case. The customers are at the store for a little retail therapy.

What's a good way to get good and happy before your shift? There's tons of self-help and warm fuzzy books to help you make a breakthrough. Or you could call a shrink on the radio for free advice. But that's not your generation's healing method. You merely need to recall the sound advice of your high school ball coach when you got injured during the game. "Rub some dirt in it and walk it off," he'd shout. Would you want to hear a laundry list of what's not going right in a People Greeter's life? Rub some dirt in it and walk it off is what you'd tell them. You can get back to the pain when your shift is over.

What about the anger you might feel from annoying coworkers and customers? There's a chance you can get an ulcer. People often give the advice that you should creatively disperse your built up rage at being mentally abused at work. You might want to take up pottery. A few minutes of letting the tension out by smashing clay between your fingers can be therapeutic and calming. Plus you'll have wonderful Christmas gifts for the surviving members of your family.

A bad creative way to resolve this rage is to write short stories about how you'll have your revenge on certain rude coworkers and idiotic customers. Rage fantasy fiction had a therapeutic value before the term "Going Postal" became the rage. If you foolishly put these literary events on the internet, you might find yourself being visited by the FBI. The stories will be used as evidence that you're plotting a terrorist incident in the workplace. Do you really want to end up behind iron bars for your golden years? There are benefits to being locked up in prison such as free room, food and healthcare. The bad part is that other inmates will mock you as lazy since you didn't do any real work to get convicted of conspiracy to commit a crime. All you did was talk about it. They had to really rob a bank to get their sentence. You're still going to have the stigma of being a lazy employee who doesn't perform real work. You'll get angry again with your new co-workers. You'll be trapped in a circle of hate.

For a position that is completely off the corporate power structure, the People Greeter receives an extraordinary amount of spite and disdain from customers and co-workers. Drunks passed out at bars and frozen hobos in the county morgue receive more pity from them. Why? Because the hobo is given the assumption that they had a traumatic event or a chemical dependency that led them to ruin. The drunk can't help themselves around booze since it's a family trait. What's your excuse for being a People Greeter at the end of your life? You can't be chemically dependent since you passed a drug test. You can't be mentally unstable or a severe criminal record because you got a job that has you interact with customers. Ultimately you are society's biggest fear. In their mind you are a person who played by the rules and completely failed. Their only defense to becoming you is to hate you. As if that really works.

A People Greeter requires thick skin, a psyche that can ignore insults and a smile that lasts the entire shift. You must achieve these three traits. You're there to brighten up the customers shopping experience and not make them feel the hate others inflict on you. Can you project sunshine on a dark day?

POP QUIZ

1) What's the fastest thing you know of?

   A. Light

   B. Thought

   C. Diarrhea

   D. Blink

   E. That joke isn't funny.

2) What should you do when insulted by co-workers?

   A. Rip into their mothers.

   B. Plot revenge.

   C. Forget about them.

   D. Slash their car tires.

3) Why would a co-worker hate you?

   A. They know your job is their fate.

   B. Jealous of your high profile position.

   C. Because they're a moron.

   D. They can't accept love.

4) What daring job should be your role model?

   A. Fire Fighter.

   B. Rodeo Clown.

   C. Dunking Booth Goon.

   D. Lion Tamer.

5) The best way to keep from being punched by a customer is?

   A. Pack a concealed weapon.

   B. Punch first.

   C. Pack a taser.

   D. Never allow yourself to be boxed in.

6) What should you do when a customer insults you?

   A. Sucker punch them as they exit.

   B. Make a joke about their mother.

   C. File a libel lawsuit.

   D. Ignore them.

7) If a customer objects to your holiday greeting?

   A. They're a Grinch.

   B. They're not spreading holiday cheer.

   C. They really need to get a life.

   D. Send them to Customer Service.

8) Best way to keep your smile during your shift is?

    A. Electroshock therapy.

    B. Primal scream therapy.

    C. Retail therapy.

    D. Rub some dirt on it and walk it off.

ANSWER KEY

1) **E.** - Just don't threaten to punch them.

2) **C.** - They're all just jealous.

3) **A.** - They merely fear becoming you.

4) **D.** - Don't bring a whip and gun to work.

5) **D.** - Keep your back away from the wall.

6) **D.** - Don't ever let them get to you.

7) **D.** - Customer Service is the best revenge.

8) **D.** - Always listen to the old ball coach's advice.

SECRET SEVEN: THIS IS THE LAST JOB YOU'LL EVER HAVE

You are born with hope. Hope fuels the optimism that your future will be brighter than a thousand suns. Hope was the key to your earlier successes. Your parents, relatives, real friends and good teachers empower the hope within you to strive for higher goals. You're always told by others to never give up hope. Nothing will be as bleak as it seem as long as you have hope in your soul.

You're trained to always hope for last minute miracles. Cowboy movies always had the good guy arrive at the last minute to save the day. Sports emphasize underdog teams making a game winning score right before the clock hit all zeroes. We maintain hope no matter how dark things become. If a tornado plows through your neighborhood, you'll hope it misses your house. We're eager to hear stories of people who are saved by miracles. Hope is ingrained into our nature. People get rich offering to reinforce your hope whether they be psychics, inspirational speakers, religious ministers or investment counselors. Hope flows through our veins like the Mississippi River.

Right now you are filled with hope even as your job prospects dwindle. You hope the phone will ring before this sentence ends. Did it? Probably not. What were you expecting to hear on the other end of the line? Who do you hope will call you right now? Perhaps you hope it's your old boss letting you know they made a major mistake by laying you off. They need you back immediately. Or do you hope your financial advisor calls with the fantastic news that a computer error made it appear that your 401K had hit rock bottom. You're really rich with plenty of cash to keep you comfortable for all the golden years. Are those your hopes every time the phone rings?

There's nothing wrong with having hope. Hope allows you to survive. Hope inspires you to thrive. Hope is what put astronauts on the moon and waffles in the toaster. Hope is what makes you answer that phone with a happy voice instead of expressing the frustration that lurks within you. You sense that things are going to turn around because hope elevates the impossible. Hope allows you to think that this is merely a bump in your upward career path. Hope insists you'll be back at your old desk or a better position shortly. However such hope will be troublesome when you seriously consider applying to be the Walmart People Greeter.

Why? Because being a Walmart People Greeter isn't a job that you can perform while waiting for your real career to restart. Decades ago when you were fresh out of college, you might have waited tables, delivered pizzas or taught as a substitute instructor. Those were perfectly fine jobs for people waiting for the right opportunity. Nobody in those positions thought that this was the perfect job to perform for the rest of their lives. These entry level jobs allowed you to show future employers that you were actively employed and not merely mooching off your parents. Your boss at the restaurant didn't get upset if your resume was being mailed out for positions that had real salaries, health insurance that could cover an actual illness and a retirement plan that wasn't a two for one large pizza coupon. Those temporary positions were truly temporary until you got on the first rung of a career ladder that continued upward to the executive washroom.

Where are you on that ladder at this moment? Has your climb hit a minor stall or a major stop? Did you lose your grip on the rung and tumble to the ground? It's hard to tell. Hope will make you sense that this is minor stall. Hope will inspire you to believe you can skip the trouble rung to end up higher than before you were pink slipped. Is hope lying to you? Are you holding onto the ladder or clinging to denial?

How can you tell if your career has hit the end of the line? There are easy ways to diagnose your true situation. Were you getting unsolicited calls from contacts at rival companies after word of your layoff got out? Did they merely offer you their condolences or were they interested in having you talk to their boss about coming over to their team? Did they actually get you an appointment with their boss or merely promise to forward your resume? Did headhunters immediately flood your voicemail upon your resume hitting the internet? Did they see you as a hot prospect that's ready to make the leap to a bigger corporation for a full time position with a major bump in salary? Or did you merely get a few emails querying if you'd be interested in taking a one month contract for a reduced salary and no benefits? Did your resume only attract positive responses from companies with exciting opportunities that involve constant travel and a salary based on 100 percent commission after an extensive non-compensated training period? Did you ever hope for a life on the road paying all your business expenses including gas and hotels with the hopes the home office will send your commission check promptly? Maybe you answered phone calls from the CEOs of start-up companies desiring your talents. It sounds promising until they mention you'd receive a deferred salary only payable if the company can achieve an IPO on the stock exchange.

Hope makes you want to see all those opportunities as golden. There's no denying the unlimited upside when compared to being a People Greeter. The 100% commission position might allow you to finally be the greatest salesman ever. The IPO offer could make you as rich as early employees of legendary websites. Reality points out that there's very little upside for you in the present tense. You only get paid after you've made them money.

Your bills won't accept future earnings as a payment option. You could waste months of your life on a someone else's collapsing dream. While the contract work pays regularly, your healthcare will be coming straight out of your pocket on a high individual rate. Since you might not be there in the next month, the company doesn't want to bother including you on their group insurance policy. Things won't be easy no matter what hope filled opportunity you take. You'll be used and abused like a rented mule since you're not really the future of the company. You're the old employee even if you're the newest hire. How hopeful are you about these future job prospects now?

Do these offers make you more eager to fill out the application to be a Walmart People Greeter? The pay scale of a Greeter won't match the lure of an unlimited commission opportunity. However as Greeter you won't waste an entire day with zero sales leading to zero commissions. You can't get a nutritious meal out of business cards and an empty gas tank. When your shift of welcoming has ended, you clock out for a paycheck. You can even use your employee discount to get a satisfying dinner to take home. You don't have to spend your nights fearing that you can't meet your weekly quota and will be fired in the morning. Can your aging body really handle the stress of a meaningless position at a heartless corporation that treats you as a series of numbers? Wouldn't you hope for a more relaxing job to allow your golden years to be shiny times?

You might be willing to apply for the People Greeter position, but are you ready? Here's a simple test: Do you have hope that being a People Greeter will merely be a temporary position until the job market turns around for you?

"No" means you're a perfect candidate for the position.

"Yes" means you're not ready to apply for the job. This is a job where the hope of returning to your old career will work against you as an employee. You have to embrace the mindset that being a People Greeter is the last job you'll ever have or it might be the last job you'll never have.

"Abandon hope all ye who enter here" was written at the entrance of Hell in Dante's *Inferno*. In a sense, this should be written above the manager's office when you apply for the People Greeter position at Walmart. That's not to say that you are doomed to eternal flames when you step inside the automatic doors for your first day on the job. You need to accept that there is no need to hope that you'll return to your former career path. Think of the times you were involved in interviewing a person for a position at your old company. Did you approve of hiring them if you sensed they were hoping to get an offer from a "better" company? You wanted a co-worker that wanted to be there. If your company wanted a temporary employee, they'd rent a person from a temporary employment agency. They wanted someone who asked if they get a gold watch when they retire from the company. Nobody wants to hire, process and train a short timer. A Walmart Manager wants to hire a person who truly desires to be a People Greeter. They will sense if your true hope isn't landing this job, but returning to your old job. You don't need to read the form letter declaring that you're overqualified for the position of People Greeter.

This powerful level of hope will work against you if you get the job. Your off-hours will be a fruitless waste of checking job listings on the internet and emailing out your resume. While getting ready for your shift, you'll burn time staring at the phone with the expectation that the next ring will be the miracle call. You'll drive to work preoccupied with the fantasy that this is the day your cellphone will ring and you'll be taking the exit that leads to your old office. At Walmart, you'll look through the incoming customers and imagine your old boss coming to rescue you. They'll pick you up and carry you into the parking lot so you can be whisked in a limo back to your old desk. Does this really ever happen? How many days can you take these hopeful fantasies dominating your waking hours? The automatic doors will evolve into a frustrating gateway to alleged career freedom. Hope will work against you every day that your cellphone doesn't vibrate with a job offer during a shift. You'll despise your life every time you check your email and only get spam. You'll despise leaving the store with the knowledge that you're not back in the game. You're just going home for another night of hoping that the salvation call will ring before you punch the clock.

You might think a rabid fan should give up hope when their team loses a big game. They should accept the fact that their team wasn't the winner. Instead the fan remains hopeful that eventually an official's rulings will be overturned or a player will be declared illegal. This happens all the time in sports. Think of the numerous Olympians who have received gold medals years after their race when the original winner is exposed for using performance enhancing drugs. College basketball teams' championship banners have been yanked from the rafters after being busted as a dirty program. A fan's unfathomable hope in the face of a harsh truth can be rewarded, which is part of why a person just can't give up hope that they will be back at their old office desk in the morning. It does happen, but will it happen to you?

The law dictating the conservation of energy declares that energy can neither be created nor destroyed. Consider hope the energy inside you. Those that are naturally full of hope can't ever truly give up hope. Merely asking you to stop hope is an impossible task. This action is as difficult as strangling yourself to death. No matter how close you get, you pass out, lose your grip and start breathing again. Hope makes you survive.

What can you do to keep hope from ruining your chances of being a People Greeter? The first thing is to not feel as if this is the worst thing that could have ever happened to you. Hope becomes more powerful in the face of desperation. Becoming a People Greeter is not the same as an addict hitting rock bottom. This is not where you intended your career track to end. The harsh truth is your career track dead ended after you received your pink slip and didn't immediately get a major job offer from a rival company. Hope will keep you endlessly circling that dead end thinking it's just a matter of time before offers overwhelm you. Don't let hope make you feel like entering Walmart for your interview is the same as a death row prisoner heading to the electric chair. Don't hope that the governor will be calling with a pardon right before the executioner flips the switch. Although in your case it would be your old boss calling your cellphone before the Walmart manager offers you the People Greeter position. This isn't that gloomy and dramatic of a situation. A part of you will not die if you accept the job. The most important quality of a People Greeter is a happy disposition. How can you radiate happiness if you're hoping to be saved from an execution?

Refocus Hope

How can you make hope work for you in the pursuit of becoming a People Greeter? You need a hope refocusing exercise. Embrace the positive elements of the People Greeter position that appeal to you. Visualize what you desire as the bright parts of future days. Picture in your mind smiling kids, gracious customers and an employee discount. Imagine the joy of not having to take your work home with you after clocking out. Think about all the horrible aspects of your old job. Reflect upon the memory of long hours, the lack of appreciation, the constant struggles with your supervisors and the painful process of when they gave you the pink slip. Reflect on how they already fired you once and they'd fire you again. You care more about them than they ever cared about you. Don't make excuses why your former employer treated you like a worthless dog. Do this exercise whenever you have a free moment or when you look at the phone expecting your old boss to call with great news. Close your eyes and do it right now. What does this moment of inner focus accomplish? You should start feeling a little different. You'll feel more depressed at the prospect of returning to your former life. The hope deep inside will work itself away from the desire for returning to your old job to anticipating the new life of a People Greeter. Hope will embrace the future instead of clinging to the past. You won't feel like a dead man walking when you arrive at Walmart to declare that you want the job.

Filling out that application for People Greeter isn't the end of your life, but the liberation of your new self. The nature of the job allows time to do things like become a great grandparent, finally fix odd items around the house and see your spouse in the daylight. You can dedicate afternoon hours to sitting on the porch and shouting at kids to get off your lawn.

Isn't that a future you'd hope for as you near complete retirement? What's holding you back from that lifestyle is the hope that you'll return to the old job. The old job doesn't offer much time to enjoy yourself and relax. Are you still hoping to return to the past? Double your efforts on the hope refocusing exercise. Refresh your memory with the frustrating long hours without overtime pay. Remind yourself of the times duties of fired co-workers piling up on your desk. Can your body still feel the stress of the days, weeks or months of waiting to know if you were part of the rumored staff cuts? Why does hope persist in wanting you to return to that old office? Does hope fear that you'll end up on a job ladder that's really a stool?

The Rung Above

Contrary to what many have said, being a Walmart People Greeter is not a dead end position. There is a reason to hope that you can move up in the job world. A major leap could be a part of your future if you can dream big. How big of a job can be above People Greeter? The skill set required as a People Greeter prepares you to be the Vice President of the United States of America. How can this be true? There's plenty of elements in your daily duties that correspond with a Vice President's Constitutional chores. You possess the ability to warmly greet foreign dignitaries and regular citizens. You're more welcoming than the Statue of Liberty. You understand how to direct foreign trading partners to the great bounty of items offered by American companies. You're an expert in projecting the perception of being in charge when in fact you're relativity powerless in your responsibilities. Vice President only has to really work to break tie votes in the senate and if the president is incapacitated. How often does that happen? You understand the major rule of never embarrassing your boss or store. A vice president's job is to never distract from the president.

Being number two at the White House is the perfect job for any People Greeter pondering a future after Walmart. You might even be overqualified to serve as Vice President. Although it would probably not be a good thing to discuss your future plans of being Vice President when interviewed for the People Greeter position. As you should know at this point, it's never good to discuss politics at a future workplace.

There's nothing wrong with hoping the People Greeter position is the last job you'll ever have. That does not mean this is the end of your life. A People Greeter is a perfect position for transitioning from a full time job to being a full time retiree. The position includes minimal pressure, no heavy lifting, keeps your mind active and allows you to maintain a happy attitude. Aren't those the qualities you'd hope to have in the last job you'll ever work?

POP QUIZ

1) Is People Greeter the last job you'll ever have?

   A. Yes.

   B. No.

   C. Maybe.

2) What's the worst thing to bring to a People Greeter job interview?

   A. The flu.

   B. Brownies.

   C. Hope that your old boss will hire you back.

   D. Pictures of your grandkids.

3) The moment your career track dead ended was:

   A. Charges were pressed.

   B. You moved back in with your parents.

   C. The minute a rival company refused to hire you.

   D. Never.

4) The job a people greeter is qualified to have is:

   A. Baseball Manager.

   B. District Regional Supervisor.

   C. Vice President of the United States of America.

   D. Radio DJ.

5) The best way to deal with hope for your old job is:

   A. Kill it.

   B. Refocus it on the joy of being a People Greeter.

   C. Admit you're a lost cause.

   D. Swear you won't settle for anything except your old job.

6) The People Greeter job is great for

   A. Transitioning into full retirement.

   B. Getting your blood pressure racing.

   C. Having you scream in public.

   D. Not caring about humanity.

7) Being a People Greeter represents:

   A. Losing all hope.

   B. The end of your career track.

   C. A little piece of you dying.

   D. A liberation of your new self.

ANSWER KEY

1) **A.** - Did you not read this chapter?

2) **C.** - You old job is in your past.

3) **C.** - This is a harsh ending to your illustrious career.

4) **C.** - You get free use of a jumbo jet.

5) **B.** - Let hope power your smile.

6) **A.** - You didn't want to drop dead at your old desk.

7) **D.** - Enjoy the change of pace.

FINAL EXAM

The final exam should not be taken alone. You need to have a friend present in the room to proctor the final exam.

While you will have an open book before you to take the final exam, this is not an open book final exam. You may not refer to any previous chapters if you can't answer a question. Your friend must have a clear view of you and the book to make sure you don't get tempted to double check your answers.

You should answer the questions using a No. 2 pencil in case you need to retake the test at a later date.

You have 30 minutes from when you turn the page to completely answer all the questions. Hand the book to your friend when you have come to the end of the questions and feel confident in your answers. Your friend will compare your answers to the answer key. They will inform of your score and its meaning.

You may turn the page and proceed to answer the final exam questions.

Joseph Corey III

FINAL EXAM QUESTIONS

The following are True or False questions.

Circle the correct answer.

1) I am a People Person.

    True or False

2) I am welcoming to strangers.

    True or False

3) I enjoy being the face of a store.

    True or False

4) I can directions to any item in the store.

    True or False

5) I can be social without socializing.

    True or False

6) I can maintain a smile under bad circumstances.

    True or False

7) I want my last job to be as a People Greeter.

    True or False

Now close the book and hand it to your friend so they can mark your answers and determine your grade.

FINAL EXAM ANSWERS

1) True

2) True

3) True

4) True

5) True

6) True

7) True

SCORING:

0-6 correct answers: You're not ready to apply for the People Greeter position.

7 correct answers: You're ready to fill out the application to be a People Greeter. Good luck.

ABOUT THE AUTHOR

Joseph Corey III is a graduate of NC State, NCSA and Glick University. His awards winning columns have appeared in newspapers, magazines, fax on demand publications and internet websites. He has been featured on the CBS news program *48 Hours* and *The Today Show*. He has also worked at numerous retail stores.

Made in the USA
Charleston, SC
28 February 2013